6/08

# Warman's
## FIELD GUIDE
to
# Precious Moments®
## Collectibles

## Values and Identification

©2007 Krause Publications

Published by

**krause publications**
*An Imprint of F+W Publications*

700 East State Street • Iola, WI 54990-0001
715-445-2214 • 888-457-2873
www.krausebooks.com

Our toll-free number to place an order or obtain a free catalog is (800) 258-0929.

The Precious Moments name is a trademark of the Precious Moments Co. Inc. and is used in this book solely for identification purposes. The Precious Moments Co. Inc. assumes no responsibility for the contents of this book. Neither the author nor the publisher are sponsored by or associated with the Precious Moments Co. Inc. or its affiliates. This book is a result of the author's independent research reporting on the secondary market and is intended to provide information for collectors.

Library of Congress Control Number: 2007924550

ISBN-13: 978-0-89689-607-9
ISBN-10: 0-89689-607-2

Designed by Donna Mummery
Edited by Mary Sieber
Photography by Doug Mitchel

Printed in China

# Contents

# Loving, Caring and Sharing— The Cornerstone of Precious Moments for 30+ Years

The Precious Moments line of collectibles began more than 30 years ago when artist Sam Butcher and his partner, Bill Biel, started a greeting card company called Jonathan & David Inc. in Grand Rapids, Michigan. They prepared a line of cards and posters with teardrop-eyed children and inspirational messages, called Precious Moments, for the Christian Booksellers Association convention in 1975.

Around that time, Eugene Freedman, then president and CEO of Enesco Corporation, spotted Butcher's artwork and thought the drawings would translate well into figurines. Japanese sculptor Yasuhei Fujioka transformed one of Butcher's drawings into three-dimensional form, and this piece was called Love One Another. Everyone was so pleased with the resulting figurine that 20 more drawings were given to the sculptor, and in 1979, 21 Precious Moments figurines (called the "Original 21") were introduced to the public. Made

*Artist Sam Butcher is the inspiration behind the Precious Moments line of collectibles.*

of porcelain bisque painted pastel colors, the figurines and their inspirational messages were an immediate hit with the public.

So popular was the line of figurines that it spawned several clubs, including the Precious Moments Collectors' Club in 1981, the Precious Moments Birthday Club in 1985, and the Precious Moments Fun Club (which replaced the Birthday Club) in 1998.

Since 1979, more than 1,500 Precious Moments figurines have been produced. Each year approximately 25 to 40 new items are released and 12 to 20 existing pieces are retired or suspended from production.

Besides the Precious Moments line, Butcher produced a collection modeled after his grandchildren, called Sammy's Circus. In 1992 he created Sugar Town, a representation of small-town life.

Today the Precious Moments collection includes figurines, ornaments, plates, bells, musicals, picture frames, and a whole host of giftware and home décor items. Enesco Corporation produced the line until 2005. Precious Moments Inc., based in Carthage, Missouri, currently oversees the distribution of Precious Moments products.

Butcher also built a chapel and theme park in Carthage, which are both open to the public. More than 10 million people have visited the Precious Moments Chapel since it opened in 1989. Each year collectors are welcome to attend two Precious Moments events at the theme park. The first is held in July and the second one is held in December.

# Original 21

Come Let Us Adore
   Him E2011

God Loveth a Cheerful
   Giver E1378

God Understands E1379B

He Careth For You E1377B

He Leadeth Me E1377A

His Burden is Light E1380G

Jesus is Born E2012

Jesus is the Answer E1381

Jesus is the Light E1373G

Jesus Loves Me (two
   figurines) E1372B
   and E1372G

Love is Kind E1379A

Love Lifted Me E1375A

Love One Another E1376

Make a Joyful Noise
   E1374G

O, How I Love
   Jesus E1380B

Praise the Lord
   Anyhow E1374B

Prayer Changes
   Things E1375B

Smile, God Loves
   You E1373B

Unto Us a Child is
   Born E2013

We Have Seen His
   Star E2010

God Loveth a Cheerful Giver E1378, 1979, **$798.**

His Burden is Light E1380G,
1979, **$85-$160.**

Jesus Loves Me E1372G,
1979, **$45-$130.**

Love One Another E1376, 1979, **$50-$120.**

Love Lifted Me E1375A, 1979, **$60-$140.**

Make a Joyful Noise E1374G, 1979, **$60-$100.**

O, How I Love Jesus
E1380B, 1979, **$85-$140.**

Praise the Lord Anyhow
E1374B, 1979, **$65-$110.**

Smile, God Loves You E1373B,
1979, **$40-$95.**

# Production Marks

A symbol or mark is found on the bottom of each Precious Moments collectible, indicating the year it was produced. Enesco Corporation began putting these marks on Precious Moments pieces starting in 1981. Figurines produced before mid-1981 have no marks and are referred to as "no mark" pieces.

The earliest marks are often the most difficult to locate and, as a result, are continually sought after by collectors. They often have a higher secondary market value as well.

| | | | |
|---|---|---|---|
| 1981 | Triangle | 1995 | Ship |
| 1982 | Hourglass | 1996 | Heart |
| 1983 | Fish | 1997 | Sword |
| 1984 | Cross | 1998 | Eyeglasses |
| 1985 | Dove | 1999 | Star |
| 1986 | Olive branch | 2000 | Cracked egg |
| 1987 | Cedar tree | 2001 | Sandal |
| 1988 | Flower | 2002 | Cross in heart |
| 1989 | Bow and arrow | 2003 | Crown |
| 1990 | Flame | 2004 | Three-petal flower |
| 1991 | Vessel | 2005 | Loaf of bread |
| 1992 | G clef | 2006 | House |
| 1993 | Butterfly | 2007 | Hammer |
| 1994 | Trumpet | | |

# How Prices Are Determined

The teardrop-eyed children and inspirational messages of Precious Moments have delighted people around the world for years. To Precious Moments aficionados, their collections are worth great sentimental value. But what are they worth in dollars and cents? To arrive at that answer, you first have to study the secondary market.

The secondary market is the market collectibles enter after they have left the original, primary point of retail sales. This market exists because a buyer is searching for an item no longer available through regular retail distribution channels. Secondary market transactions are represented by sales between individual collectors as well as dealers who may or may not be involved with primary retail selling.

Because secondary market prices can vary from region to region, and even within a given locale, values listed in *Warman's Field Guide to Precious Moments Collectibles* are simply guides to help collectors, insurance agents, appraisers, and others determine the "going" or "asking" price. These values reflect the most often asked-for or sold-for prices. *Warman's Field Guide to Precious Moments Collectibles* is not published to determine exact pricing information on Precious Moments and should not be taken as such.

Inside this book you'll find secondary market values for more than 3,000 Precious Moments collectibles from 1978 through 2007. The prices published here are average or fair trend values at which the items, in mint condition and with their original boxes, are currently trading hands. Several steps were taken to arrive at these prices. This included researching everything available on Precious Moments: reading other books on collectibles; studying Internet auctions; working with secondary market dealers and exchange specialists; and talking with readers and collectors.

Oftentimes a specific Precious Moments item was made for more than just one year. Check your item's production mark or symbol, usually located on the bottom or underside of the piece, to determine which year it was produced (see "Production Marks"). Usually an item produced during an earlier year of its production run is worth more than the same piece produced during a later year. In some of the photograph captions you'll notice price ranges. Generally, if your collectible has an earlier bottom mark, it's worth the higher price; if it has a later bottom mark, it's worth the lower price. Be sure to check the secondary market listings for more information.

In some instances, I was able to determine specific values for pieces produced during different years and with different bottom marks. In those cases I indicate the appropriate bottom mark in parentheses ( ), which appears after the title of the piece.

Precious Moments pieces signed by Sam Butcher may be worth more than unsigned pieces. If your item is signed by Butcher, it may be worth approximately 10-20 percent more than the value listed.

If you no longer have the original box an item was packaged in, deduct $5 to $10 from the price listed to determine the value of your collectible.

*Please keep in mind this book is simply a guide to be used in conjunction with every other bit of information you can obtain to determine a realistic value for your Precious Moments collectibles. In the end, enthusiasts like you determine the true value of Precious Moments when you actively buy and sell them on the secondary market.*

# How to Use This Book

*Warman's Field Guide to Precious Moments Collectibles* is divided into four sections by collectible type: bells, figurines, ornaments, and plates. Within these categories, the listings are arranged in alphabetical order according to the item's name. These listings include:

- title (name) of the piece
- identifying number
- series in which the item appeared (if applicable)
- year the piece was first issued
- edition size or status; and
- current secondary market trend price

The following abbreviations are used to indicate edition size or status of a piece:

CL  = closed edition (item no longer being produced)

OP  = open edition (item produced in an unlimited quantity)

RT  = retired edition (item no longer produced and mold destroyed)

SU  = suspended edition (production of item temporarily ceased)

LE  = limited edition (item is produced in a specific quantity but quantity is unknown at this time)

YR  = year edition (item produced for one year only)

\*   = Unknown

N/A = not available

Each photograph is fully identified with the name of the piece, the year it was first produced, the series in which it appeared (if applicable), and its current secondary market value.

# Helpful Websites

To learn more about the Precious Moments line, or to buy and/or sell Precious Moments collectibles, visit the following Internet sites:

preciousmoments.com (official Precious Moments website)
gocollect.com
collectiblestoday.com
preciousmomentscommunity.com
preciousmomentsonline.com
cherrylanecollection.com
heritagegiftstore.com
allensinc.com
ebay.com
europeanimports.com
collectibles-crazy.com
darlingdears.com

# Special Thanks

This book would have never existed without the help of Precious Moments collectors Pam Scott, Sue Scott, and Patti Basso of southern Wisconsin. This trio of collectors truly personified the Precious Moments theme of "loving, caring, and sharing" by graciously welcoming us into their homes to photograph their collections, and then answering countless questions about them for this book. We couldn't have done it without them!

# Bells

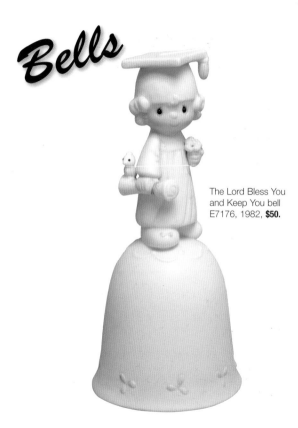

The Lord Bless You and Keep You bell E7176, 1982, **$50.**

# BELLS

| Title | Series | Limit | Trend |
|-------|--------|-------|-------|
| But the Greatest of These Is Love 527726, 1992 | Annual Bells | CL | **$18** |
| Girl With Patchwork Quilt 4003311, 2005 | Various Bells | OP | **$25** |
| God Sent His Love 15873, 1985 | Annual Bells | CL | **$23** |
| God Understands E5211, 1980 | Various Bells | RT | **$40** |
| House of Bells Vignette, set of 3, 879614, 2003 | Various Bells | RT | **$85** |
| I'll Play My Drum For Him E2358, 1982 | Annual Bells | YR | **$74** |
| Jesus Is Born E5623, 1980 | Various Bells | SU | **$44** |
| Jesus Loves Me E5208, 1980 | Various Bells | SU | **$39** |
| Jesus Loves Me E5209, 1980 | Various Bells | SU | **$46** |
| Let the Heavens Rejoice E5622, 1980 | Annual Bells | YR | **$175** |
| Lord Bless You and Keep You, The E7175, 1981 | Various Bells | SU | **$27** |
| Lord Bless You and Keep You, The E7176, 1982 | Various Bells | SU | **$50** |
| Lord Bless You and Keep You, The E7179, 1982 | Various Bells | SU | **$65** |

| Title | Series | Limit | Trend |
|-------|--------|-------|-------|
| Love Is the Best Gift of All<br>109835, 1987 | Annual Bells | YR | **$25** |
| Make Your Holidays Sparkle<br>104056, 2002 | Various Bells | CL | **$30** |
| May Your Christmas Be Merry<br>524182, 1991 | Annual Bells | SU | **$23** |

The Lord Bless You and Keep You bell E7179, 1982, **$65.**

The Purr-Fect Grandma bell E7183, 1982, **$32.**

| Title | Series | Limit | Trend |
|---|---|---|---|
| Mother Sew Dear E7181, 1981 | Various Bells | SU | **$29** |
| Oh Holy Night 522821, 1988 | Annual Bells | CL | **$28** |
| Once Upon a Holy Night 523828, 1989 | Annual Bells | CL | **$22** |
| Prayer Changes Things E5210, 1980 | Various Bells | SU | **$38** |
| Purr-fect Grandma, The E7183, 1982 | Various Bells | SU | **$32** |
| S'mitten With the Christmas Spirit 117845, 2004 | Various Bells | YR | **$10** |
| Surrounded With Joy E0522, 1983 | Annual Bells | YR | **$45** |
| Time to Wish You a Merry Christmas 115304, 1988 | Annual Bells | CL | **$33** |
| We Have Seen His Star E5620, 1981 | Various Bells | SU | **$41** |
| Wishing You a Cozy Christmas 102318, 1985 | Annual Bells | CL | **$22** |
| Wishing You a Merry Christmas E5393, 1984 | Annual Bells | YR | **$28** |
| Wishing You the Sweetest Christmas 530174, 1993 | Various Bells | YR | **$29** |

# *Figurines*

Age 1 136190, Growing in Grace, 1995, **$23.**

# FIGURINES

| Title | Series | Limit | Trend |
|---|---|---|---|
| 15 Happy Years Together, What a Tweet! 530786, 1993 | 15th Anniversary | YR | **$119** |
| 16 & Feline Fine 116948, 2004 | Birthday Train | OP | **$25** |
| 20 Years and the Vision's Still the Same 306843, 1998 | Collectors' Club | SU | **$64** |
| 4-H Power of Youth, The 110271, 2002 | Chapel Exclusive | OP | **$30** |
| Adopting a Life of Love 108527, 2003 | General Line | OP | **$45** |
| Afri-can Be There For You I Will Be (Kenya) 456462, 1998 | Little Moments International | OP | **$35** |
| Age 1 136190, 1995 | Growing In Grace | OP | **$23** |
| Age 10 183873, 1996 | Growing In Grace | OP | **$31** |
| Age 11 260924, 1997 | Growing In Grace | OP | **$36** |
| Age 12 260932, 1997 | Growing In Grace | OP | **$35** |
| Age 13 272647, 1997 | Growing In Grace | OP | **$36** |
| Age 14 272655, 1997 | Growing In Grace | OP | **$32** |
| Age 15 272663, 1997 | Growing In Grace | OP | **$36** |
| Age 16 136263, 1995 | Growing In Grace | OP | **$38** |
| Age 2 136212, 1995 | Growing In Grace | OP | **$23** |

Age 2 136212, Growing in
Grace, 1995, **$23.**

Age 3 136220, Growing in
Grace, 1995, **$23.**

Age 4 136239, Growing in
Grace, 1995, **$27.**

Age 5 136247, Growing in
Grace, 1995, **$27.**

Age 6
136255,
Growing in
Grace, 1995,
**$27.**

Age 7 163740,
Growing in Grace,
1995, **$32.**

Age 9 183865, Growing in Grace, 1996, **$27.**

Alaska Once More, How's Yer Christmas? 455784, 1998, **$31.**

| Title | Series | Limit | Trend |
|-------|--------|-------|-------|
| Age 3 136220, 1995 | Growing In Grace | OP | **$23** |
| Age 4 136239, 1995 | Growing In Grace | OP | **$27** |
| Age 5 136247, 1995 | Growing In Grace | OP | **$27** |
| Age 6 136255, 1995 | Growing In Grace | OP | **$27** |
| Age 6 136255B, 1995 | Growing In Grace | OP | **$27** |
| Age 7 163740, 1995 | Growing In Grace | OP | **$32** |
| Age 8 163759, 1995 | Growing In Grace | OP | **$32** |
| Age 9 183865, 1996 | Growing In Grace | OP | **$27** |
| Alaska Once More, How's Yer Christmas? 455784, 1998 | General Line | OP | **$31** |
| All Aboard For Birthday Club Fun B0007, 1992 | Birthday Club | CL | **$30** |
| All Aboard For Birthday Club Fun B0107, 1992 | Birthday Club | CL | **$34** |
| All About Heaven 525952, 2001 | Mini Nativity | OP | **$18** |
| All Done 630023, 2007 | Picture Perfect Moments | OP | **$20** |
| All Girls Are Beautiful 481661, 1998 | General Line | CL | **$60** |
| All Sing His Praises 184012, 1996 | Nativity | SU | **$30** |

| Title | Series | Limit | Trend |
|---|---|---|---|
| All Things Grow With Love 139505, 1996 | Little Moments | OP | **$20** |
| All Wrapped Up With Love 117795, 2004 | Hark the Heavens | 10000 | **$40** |
| Alleluia, He Is Risen 108525, 2003 | General Line | OP | **$36** |
| Alleluia, He Is Risen 692409, 2000 | General Line | SU | **$30** |
| Allow Sunshine & Laughter to Fill Your Day 4001785, 2005 | Century Circle Carousel | 2000 | **$75** |
| Always By Your Side (Boy) 550023, 2006 | General Line | OP | **$45** |
| Always By Your Side (Girl) 550022, 2006 | General Line | OP | **$45** |
| Always Close to My Heart 4001645, 2005 | General Line | OP | **$34** |
| Always In His Care 225290, 1990 | General Line | YR | **$12** |
| Always In His Care 524522, 1990 | Easter Seals | SU | **$38** |
| Always Listen to Your Heart 488356, 1999 | Special Wishes | SU | **$22** |
| Always On the Ball 120124, 2004 | Special Wishes | OP | **$32** |
| Always Room For One More C0009, 1989 | Collectors' Club | CL | **$30** |
| Always Room For One More C0109, 1989 | Collectors' Club | CL | **$45** |
| Always Take Time to Pray PM952, 1995 | Collectors' Club | CL | **$34** |

All Things Grow With Love 139505, Little Moments, 1996, **$20.**

Always Close to My Heart 4001645, 2005, **$34.**

| Title | Series | Limit | Trend |
|-------|--------|-------|-------|
| America, You're Beautiful 528862, 1993 | General Line | CL | **$46** |
| America, You're Beautiful 528862R, 2001 | America Forever | LE | **$35** |
| American Bison E1527, 2003 | Endangered Species | 7,500 | **$45** |
| Amethyst—Color of Faith February 335541, 1998 | Birthstone | OP | **$25** |
| And a Child Shall Lead Them E9287R, 1996 | General Line | RT | **$35** |
| And the Angels Sing 610042, 2006 | General Line | CL | **$30** |
| And to All a Good Night 104217, 2002 | Christmas Remembered | RT | **$55** |
| And You Shall See a Star 272787, 1997 | Nativity | RT | **$33** |
| Angel In Disguise, An 4001573, 2005 | Premier Collection | 3,000 | **$115** |
| Angel of Mercy 102482, 1986 | General Line | OP | **$31** |
| Angels Keep While Shepherds Sleep 4003179, 2005 | Herald Angels | YR | **$65** |
| Angels On Earth 183776, 1996 | General Line | RT | **$40** |
| Angels We Have Heard On High 524921, 1990 | General Line | RT | **$75** |
| Another Year and More Grey Hares 128686, 1995 | General Line | RT | **$24** |
| April 110027, 1988 | Calendar Girl | RT | **$78** |
| April 261300, 1996 | Little Moments Birthstone Collection | OP | **$20** |

| Title | Series | Limit | Trend |
|---|---|---|---|
| April Girl With Waterball 844306, 2001 | General Line | * | **$18** |
| Aquamarine—Color of Kindness, March 335568, 1998 | Birthstone | OP | **$25** |
| Are You Lonesome Tonight? 110262, 2003 | Animal Affections | OP | **$18** |
| Arose On Her Toes 0000383, 2005 | Special Wishes | OP | **$40** |
| August, 1997 | Little Moments | OP | **$20** |
| August 110078, 1988 | Calendar Girl | RT | **$63** |
| August 261319, 1996 | Little Moments Birthstone Collection | OP | **$20** |
| August Girl With Waterball 844349, 2001 | General Line | * | **$18** |
| Aunt Bulah and Uncle Sam 272825, 1997 | Sugar Town | RT | **$28** |
| Aunt Cleo 272817, 1997 | Sugar Town | RT | **$24** |
| Aunt Ruth and Aunt Dorothy 529486, 1992 | Sugar Town | RT | **$41** |
| Auntie, You Make Beauty Blossom 737623, 2000 | General Line | SU | **$40** |
| Autumn's Praise 12084, 1986 | Four Seasons | YR | **$50** |
| Autumn's Praise Musical 408751, 1984 | Four Seasons | LE | **$135** |
| Baby Boy Crawling E2852E, 1987 | General Line | SU | **$70** |
| Baby Boy Sitting E2852C, 1987 | General Line | SU | **$70** |
| Baby Boy Standing E2852A, 1987 | General Line | SU | **$70** |

| Title | Series | Limit | Trend |
|---|---|---|---|
| Baby Figurines 6-Pc. set E2852, 1983 | General Line | SU | **$197** |
| Baby Girl Lying Down E2852F, 1987 | General Line | SU | **$29** |
| Baby Girl Sitting E2852D, 1987 | General Line | SU | **$70** |
| Baby Girl Standing E2852B, 1987 | General Line | SU | **$70** |
| Baby Moses 649953, 1999 | Little Moments Bible Stories | YR | **$25** |
| Baby's First Birthday 524069, 1992 | Baby's First | OP | **$31** |
| Baby's First Christmas 15539, 1985 | General Line | CL | **$24** |
| Baby's First Christmas 15547, 1985 | General Line | CL | **$24** |
| Baby's First Haircut 12211, 1984 | Baby's First | SU | **$108** |
| Baby's First Meal 524077, 1990 | Baby's First | RT | **$40** |
| Baby's First Pet 520705, 1988 | Baby's First | SU | **$42** |
| Baby's First Picture E2841, 1984 | Baby's First | RT | **$110** |
| Baby's First Step E2840, 1984 | Baby's First | SU | **$80** |
| Baby's First Trip 16012, 1985 | Baby's First | SU | **$234** |
| Baby's First Word 527238, 1992 | Baby's First | RT | **$17** |
| Banner of Hope, A Symbol of Pride, A 117581, 2005 | General Line | OP | **$40** |
| Bare Necessities 620022, 2006 | Picture Perfect Moments | OP | **$20** |
| Be Fruitful and Multiply 524409, 2000 | General Line | OP | **$45** |
| Be Not Weary In Doing Well E3111, 1980 | General Line | RT | **$105** |

Autumn's Praise 12084, Four Seasons series, 1986, **$50.**

Baby Boy Crawling E2852E, 1987, **$70.**

Baby Boy
Standing
E2852A,
1987, **$70.**

Baby Girl Lying Down E2852F, 1987, **$29.**

Baby Girl Sitting E2852D, 1987, **$70.**

Baby Girl
Standing
E2852B,
1987, **$70.**

Baby's First Picture E2841, Baby's First series, 1984, **$110.**

Baby's First Word 527238, Baby's First series, 1992, **$17.**

Be Not Weary in Doing Well E3111, 1979, **$65-$185.**

| Title | Series | Limit | Trend |
|---|---|---|---|
| Be Not Weary In Doing Well E3111 (Cross Mark), 1984 | General Line | RT | **$65** |
| Be Not Weary In Doing Well E3111 (Fish Mark), 1983 | General Line | RT | **$70** |
| Be Not Weary In Doing Well E3111 (Hourglass Mark), 1982 | General Line | RT | **$75** |
| Be Not Weary In Doing Well E3111 (Title Error: Be Not Weary and Doing Well), 1979 | General Line | RT | **$185** |
| Be Not Weary In Doing Well E3111 (Triangle Mark), 1981 | General Line | RT | **$75** |
| Be Not Weary In Well Doing E3111, 1979 | General Line | RT | **$150** |
| Bear Ye One Another's Burdens E5200, 1980 | General Line | SU | **$100** |
| Bear Ye One Another's Burdens E5200 (Cross Mark), 1984 | General Line | SU | **$65** |
| Bear Ye One Another's Burdens E5200 (Fish Mark), 1983 | General Line | SU | **$70** |
| Bear Ye One Another's Burdens E5200 (Hourglass Mark), 1982 | General Line | SU | **$75** |
| Bear Ye One Another's Burdens E5200 (Triangle Mark), 1981 | General Line | SU | **$90** |
| Bearing Gifts of Great Joy 112863, 2003 | Nativity | OP | **$32** |
| Beary Loving Collector 823953, 2001 | Collectors' Club | * | **$15** |

| Title | Series | Limit | Trend |
|---|---|---|---|
| Beautiful and Blushing, My Baby's Now a Bride 117802, 2004 | General Line | OP | **$45** |
| Beauty of God Blooms Forever (Spring), The 129143, 2000 | Four Seasons | RT | **$80** |
| Behold the Lamb of God 588164, 1999 | Nativity | RT | **$45** |
| Behold the Lord (3 pieces) 737607, 2000 | General Line | OP | **$23** |
| Being Nine Is Just Divine 521833, 1992 | Birthday Train | OP | **$23** |
| Believe It Or Knot I Luv You 487910, 1999 | General Line | OP | **$30** |
| Believe the Impossible 109487, 1988 | General Line | SU | **$70** |
| Believe the Impossible 109487R, 2000 | Care-A-Van | RT | **$40** |
| Beside the Still Waters (Summer) 129127, 2000 | Four Seasons | RT | **$50** |
| Best Friends Share the Same Heart 890987, 2002 | General Line | OP | **$45** |
| Best Man (African-American) 902020, 2002 | General Line | OP | **$25** |
| Best Man (Asian) 902047, 2002 | General Line | OP | **$25** |
| Best Man (Hispanic) 901563, 2001 | General Line | SU | **$25** |
| Best Man E2836, 1984 | Bridal Party | OP | **$22** |
| Bike Rack 272906, 1997 | Sugar Town | RT | **$22** |
| Bird Bath 150223, 1995 | Sugar Town | RT | **$10** |
| Birds of a Feather Collect Together E0006, 1986 | Collectors' Club | CL | **$32** |

| Title | Series | Limit | Trend |
|---|---|---|---|
| Birds of a Feather Collect Together E0106, 1985 | Collectors' Club | CL | **$36** |
| Birthday Wishes With Hugs and Kisses 4004682, 2005 | General Line | OP | **$24** |
| Birthday Wishes With Hugs and Kisses 139556, 1996 | Little Moments | OP | **$20** |
| Bless the Days of Our Youth 16004, 1985 | Birthday Train | OP | **$23** |
| Bless This House E7164 (Cross Mark), 1984 | General Line | SU | **$205** |
| Bless This House E7164 (Fish Mark), 1983 | General Line | SU | **$240** |
| Bless This House E7164 (Hourglass Mark), 1982 | General Line | SU | **$290** |
| Bless Those Who Serve Their Country (Air Force) 526584, 1990 | General Line | SU | **$40** |
| Bless Those Who Serve Their Country (Army) 526576, 1990 | General Line | SU | **$40** |
| Bless Those Who Serve Their Country (Black) 527297, 1990 | General Line | SU | **$40** |
| Bless Those Who Serve Their Country (Girl) 527289, 1990 | General Line | SU | **$28** |
| Bless Those Who Serve Their Country (Marine) 527521, 1990 | General Line | SU | **$37** |
| Bless Those Who Serve Their Country (Navy) 526568, 1990 | General Line | SU | **$111** |
| Bless You 620021, 2006 | Picture Perfect Moments | OP | **$20** |

Believe It Or Knot, I Luv You 487910, 1999, **$30.**

Birds of a Feather Collect Together E0106, 1985, **$36.**

Five Birthday Train pieces: Happy Birthday, Little Lamb, **$15;** May Your Birthday Be Gigantic, **$19**; This Day is Something to Roar About, **$23**; Keep Looking Up, **$23**; and Isn't Eight Just Great, **$23.**

Birthday Wishes
With Hugs and
Kisses 139556,
Little Moments,
1996, **$20.**

Bless You
Two E9255,
1982, **$48.**

Blessed Are the Peacemakers E3107, 1980, **$60-$105.**

Blessed Are They That Overcome 115479, Easter Seals, 1987, **$27.**

| Title | Series | Limit | Trend |
|---|---|---|---|
| Bless You 679879, 1999 | General Line | SU | **$23** |
| Bless You Two E9255, 1982 | General Line | OP | **$48** |
| Bless Your Little Tutu 261173, 1997 | Little Moments | OP | **$20** |
| Bless Your Sole 531162, 1995 | General Line | RT | **$23** |
| Blessed Are the Meek For They Shall Inherit the Earth 523313, 1991 | Chapel Exclusive | LE | **$50** |
| Blessed Are the Merciful 523291, 1994 | Chapel Exclusive | LE | **$68** |
| Blessed Are the Merciful PM972, 1997 | Collectors' Club | CL | **$40** |
| Blessed Are the Peacemakers 523348, 1995 | Chapel Exclusive | LE | **$65** |
| Blessed Are the Peacemakers E3107, 1980 | General Line | RT | **$105** |
| Blessed Are the Peacemakers E3107 (Cross Mark), 1984 | General Line | RT | **$60** |
| Blessed Are the Peacemakers E3107 (Fish Mark), 1983 | General Line | RT | **$70** |
| Blessed Are the Peacemakers E3107 (Hourglass Mark), 1982 | General Line | RT | **$85** |
| Blessed Are the Peacemakers E3107 (Triangle Mark), 1981 | General Line | RT | **$95** |
| Blessed Are the Poor In Spirit 523437, 1992 | Chapel Exclusive | CL | **$34** |
| Blessed Are the Pure In Heart 523399, 1994 | Chapel Exclusive | CL | **$65** |
| Blessed Are the Pure In Heart E3104, 1979 | General Line | SU | **$55** |

| Title | Series | Limit | Trend |
|---|---|---|---|
| Blessed Are the Pure In Heart E3104, 1980 | General Line | SU | **$52** |
| Blessed Are the Pure In Heart E3104, 1984+ | General Line | SU | **$35** |
| Blessed Are the Pure In Heart E3104 (Fish Mark), 1983 | General Line | SU | **$45** |
| Blessed Are the Pure In Heart E3104 (Hourglass Mark), 1982 | General Line | SU | **$45** |
| Blessed Are the Pure In Heart E3104 (Triangle Mark), 1981 | General Line | SU | **$45** |
| Blessed Are They That Mourn 523380, 1992 | Chapel Exclusive | CL | **$52** |
| Blessed Are They That Overcome 115479, 1987 | Easter Seals | RT | **$27** |
| Blessed Are They Which Do Hunger to Be Filled 523321, 1991 | Chapel Exclusive | CL | **$51** |
| Blessed Are They With a Caring Heart 163724, 1999 | Century Circle | CL | **$65** |
| Blessed Are Those Who Serve 113963, 2004 | Special Wishes | OP | **$30** |
| Blessed Are Thou Amongst Women 261556, 1998 | Events | SU | **$122** |
| Blessed Be the Tie That Binds 520918, 2000 | General Line | OP | **$50** |
| Blessed With a Loving Godmother 795348, 2000 | General Line | SU | **$40** |
| Blessed With a Miracle 120110, 2004 | General Line | OP | **$50** |
| Blessed With Small Miracles PM0031A, 2003 | Collectors' Club | * | **$40** |

| Title | Series | Limit | Trend |
|---|---|---|---|
| Blessings From Above 523747, 1989 | General Line | RT | **$57** |
| Blessings From My House to Yours E0503, 1983 | General Line | SU | **$70** |
| Bless-Um You 527335, 1992 | General Line | RT | **$36** |
| Blonde Dad 848743, 2001 | Little Moments Build a Family | OP | **$20** |
| Blonde Infant Daughter 848808, 2001 | Little Moments Build a Family | OP | **$13** |
| Blonde Infant Son 848816, 2001 | Little Moments Build a Family | OP | **$28** |
| Blonde Mom 848735, 2001 | Little Moments Build a Family | OP | **$20** |
| Blonde Teen Daughter 848751, 2001 | Little Moments Build a Family | OP | **$18** |
| Blonde Teen Son 848778, 2001 | Little Moments Build a Family | OP | **$18** |
| Blonde Toddler Daughter 848786, 2001 | Little Moments Build a Family | OP | **$27** |
| Blonde Toddler Son 848794, 2001 | Little Moments Build a Family | OP | **$27** |
| Blooming In God's Love 4001245, 2004 | General Line | OP | **$50** |
| Bluebirds Musical waterglobe 631002, 2007 | Bluebirds of Happiness | OP | **$25** |
| Bon Voyage! 522201, 1988 | General Line | SU | **$110** |
| Bonfire With Bunnies 184152, 1996 | Sugar Town | RT | **$18** |
| Bottoms Up 630021, 2007 | Picture Perfect Moments | OP | **$20** |

| Title | Series | Limit | Trend |
|---|---|---|---|
| Bouquet From God's Garden of Love, A 184268, 1996 | Growing In God's Garden of Love | RT | **$35** |
| Boy Angel Messenger of Love 119837, 2004 | General Line | OP | **$20** |
| Boy Placing Star On Tree 4003327, 2005 | General Line | OP | **$43** |
| Bride (African-American) 795364, 2001 | General Line | OP | **$30** |
| Bride (Asian) 795402, 2001 | General Line | OP | **$30** |
| Bride (Caucasian Brunette) 874485, 2001 | Lord Bless You and Keep You | SU | **$50** |
| Bride (Hispanic) 795380, 2000 | General Line | SU | **$30** |
| Bride E2846, 1983 | Bridal Party | OP | **$27** |
| Bridesmaid E2831, 1984 | Bridal Party | OP | **$25** |
| Bright and Shining Moment, A, 115921, 2004 | Events | LE | **$32** |
| Brighten Someone's Day 105953, 1987 | Birthday Series | SU | **$22** |
| Bring the Little Ones to Jesus 527556, 1990 | General Line | RT | **$92** |
| Bringing God's Blessing to You E0509, 1983 | Nativity | SU | **$63** |
| Bringing In the Sheaves 307084, 1998 | Country Lane | 12,000 | **$275** |
| Bringing You a Merry Christmas 527599, 1992 | General Line | RT | **$52** |
| Bringing You My Heart 118728, 2004 | General Line | RT | **$45** |
| Bringing You the Gift of Peace 117793, 2004 | Hark the Heavens | 10,000 | **$36** |

Blessings From My House to Yours E0503, 1983, **$70.**

A Bouquet From God's Garden of Love 184268, Growing in God's Garden of Love series, 1996, **$35.**

Brighten Someone's Day 105953, Birthday series, 1987, **$22.**

| Title | Series | Limit | Trend |
|-------|--------|-------|-------|
| Brotherly Love 100544, 1985 | General Line | SU | **$70** |
| Brunette Dad 880841, 2001 | Little Moments Build a Family | OP | **$34** |
| Brunette Infant Daughter 880906, 2001 | Little Moments Build a Family | OP | **$27** |
| Brunette Infant Son 880914, 2001 | Little Moments Build a Family | OP | **$27** |
| Brunette Mom 880833, 2001 | Little Moments Build a Family | OP | **$34** |
| Brunette Teenage Daughter 880868, 2001 | Little Moments Build a Family | OP | **$18** |
| Brunette Teenage Son 880876, 2001 | Little Moments Build a Family | OP | **$30** |
| Brunette Toddler Daughter 880884, 2001 | Little Moments Build a Family | OP | **$27** |
| Brunette Toddler Son 880892, 2001 | Little Moments Build a Family | OP | **$27** |
| Bubble Your Trouble Away 101730, 2002 | Collectors' Club | * | **$45** |
| Bubbling Over With Fun FC790005, 2007 | Fun Club | * | **$25** |
| Building Special Friendships 879029, 2001 | Boys & Girls Clubs of America | YR | **$130** |
| Bundles of Joy E2374, 1984+ | General Line | RT | **$50** |
| Bundles of Joy E2374 (Fish Mark), 1983 | General Line | RT | **$85** |
| Bundles of Joy E2374 (Hourglass Mark), 1982 | General Line | RT | **$120** |

Brotherly Love 100544, 1985, **$70.**

Can't Be
Without You
524492,
Birthday
series, 1990,
**$16.**

Can't Beehive
Myself Without You
BC891, Precious
Moments Birthday
Club, 1989, **$47.**

Cheers to the Leader 104035, 1986, **$27.**

| Title | Series | Limit | Trend |
|---|---|---|---|
| Cats With Kitten 291293, 1997 | Mini Nativity | OP | **$35** |
| Caught Up In the Sweet Thoughts of You 521973, 1998 | Special Wishes | SU | **$30** |
| Celebrating His Arrival 878952, 2001 | General Line | OP | **$40** |
| Cent With Love 4001667, 2005 | General Line | OP | **$23** |
| Chapel Nightlight 529621, 1992 | Sugar Town | RT | **$114** |
| Charity Begins In the Heart 307009, 1997 | Victorian Series | RT | **$54** |
| Cheers to the Leader 104035, 1986 | General Line | RT | **$27** |
| Cherish Every Step 795224, 2001 | Motherhood | OP | **$50** |
| Cherishing Each Special Moment 101233, 2002 | Motherhood | OP | **$45** |
| Chester BC992, 1999 | Fun Club | YR | **$7** |
| Child Is a Gift of God, A 113962, 2004 | General Line | OP | **$40** |
| Chip Off the Old Block, A 110266, 2003 | Animal Affections | OP | **$18** |
| Christmas Around the World 116710, 2003 | Events | 1,100 | **$35** |

Cherishing Each Special Moment
101233, Motherhood series,
2002, **$45.**

A Collection of Precious
Moments 745510, 2000, **$27.**

Come Let Us Adore Him E2800, Nativity series, 1980, **$130-$180** .

| Title | Series | Limit | Trend |
|---|---|---|---|
| Christmas Fireplace 524883, 1990 | Family Christmas | SU | **$60** |
| Christmas Is a Time to Share E2802, 1979 | Nativity | SU | **$95** |
| Christmas Is a Time to Share E2802, 1980 | Nativity | SU | **$110** |
| Christmas Is a Time to Share E2802 (Cross Mark), 1984 | Nativity | SU | **$75** |
| Christmas Is a Time to Share E2802 (Fish Mark), 1983 | Nativity | SU | **$80** |
| Christmas Is a Time to Share E2802 (Hourglass Mark), 1982 | Nativity | SU | **$90** |
| Christmas Is a Time to Share E2806, 1980 | Musical | RT | **$180** |
| Christmas Is a Time to Share E2806 (Cross Mark), 1984 | Musical | RT | **$145** |
| Christmas Is a Time to Share E2806 (Fish Mark), 1983 | Musical | RT | **$155** |
| Christmas Is a Time to Share E2806 (Hourglass Mark), 1982 | Musical | RT | **$155** |
| Christmas Is a Time to Share E2806 (Triangle Mark), 1981 | Musical | RT | **$165** |

| Title | Series | Limit | Trend |
|-------|--------|-------|-------|
| Christmas Is Caring 610015, 2006 | General Line | OP | **$50** |
| Christmas Is Loving 610014, 2006 | General Line | OP | **$50** |
| Christmas Is Sharing 610016, 2006 | General Line | CL | **$50** |
| Christmas Joy From Head to Toe E2361, 1982 | General Line | SU | **$37** |
| Christmas Street Precious Scape 750123, 2000 | General Line | OP | **$25** |
| Christmas Trees Precious Scape 788171, 2000 | General Line | CL | **$50** |
| Christmastime Is For Sharing E0504 (Cross Mark), 1984 | General Line | RT | **$65** |
| Christmastime Is For Sharing E0504 (Fish Mark), 1983 | General Line | RT | **$105** |
| Chrysanthemum Sassy and Cheerful, November 101527, 2002 | Calendar Girl | OP | **$36** |
| Chuck 272809, 1997 | Sugar Town | YR | **$34** |
| Clown Balancing Ball 12238A, 1987 | General Line | SU | **$28** |
| Clown Bending Over Ball 12238C, 1987 | General Line | SU | **$35** |

| Title | Series | Limit | Trend |
|---|---|---|---|
| Clown Holding Balloon 12238B, 1987 | General Line | SU | **$35** |
| Clown Holding Flower Pot 12238D, 1987 | General Line | SU | **$35** |
| Clowns, set of 2 thimbles 100668, 1986 | General Line | SU | **$30** |
| Club That's Out of This World, The C0012, 1992 | Collectors' Club | CL | **$32** |
| Club That's Out of This World, The C0112, 1992 | Collectors' Club | CL | **$40** |
| Club Where Fellowship Reigns, A 635278, 2000 | Collectors' Club | CL | **$50** |
| Club Where Friendships Are Made, A 635251, 2000 | Collectors' Club | CL | **$40** |
| Coach, You're a Real Sport 112859, 2003 | Special Wishes | OP | **$30** |
| Cobblestone Bridge, 1994 | Sugar Town | RT | **$20** |
| Cocoa 184063, 1996 | Sugar Town | RT | **$17** |
| Collecting Friends Along the Way PM002, 2000 | Collectors' Club | CL | **$100** |
| Collecting Life's Most Precious Moments 108531, 2002 | 25th Anniversary | YR | **$45** |
| Collecting Makes Good Scents BC901, 1990 | Birthday Club | CL | **$24** |

Clown Balancing Ball 12238A, 1987, **$28.**

Clown Bending Over Ball 12238C, 1987, **$35.**

Clown Holding Balloon 12238B, 1987, **$35.**

Clown Holding Flower Pot 12238D, 1987, **$35.**

| Title | Series | Limit | Trend |
|---|---|---|---|
| Collection of Precious Moments, A 731129, 1999 | General Line | OP | **$25** |
| Collection of Precious Moments, A 745510, 2000 | General Line | RT | **$27** |
| Collin 529214, 1993 | Sammy's Circus | SU | **$16** |
| Color Your World With Thanksgiving 183857, 1996 | General Line | RT | **$36** |
| Come Let Us Adore Him (set of 9) E2800, 1980 | Nativity | DS | **$180** |
| Come Let Us Adore Him (set of 9) E2800, 1984-1985 | Nativity | DS | **$130** |
| Come Let Us Adore Him (set of 9) E2800 (Fish Mark), 1983 | Nativity | DS | **$135** |
| Come Let Us Adore Him (set of 9) E2800 (Hourglass Mark), 1982 | Nativity | DS | **$140** |
| Come Let Us Adore Him (set of 9) E2800 (Triangle Mark), 1981 | Nativity | DS | **$155** |
| Come Let Us Adore Him 104000 (set of 9), 1986 | Nativity | OP | **$112** |
| Come Let Us Adore Him 104523, 1986 | Nativity | CL | **$465** |

Come Let Us Adore Him 104000, Nativity series, 1986, **$112.**

Cosmos, "Ambitious," October 101526, Calendar Girl series, 2002, **$36.**

| Title | Series | Limit | Trend |
|---|---|---|---|
| Come Let Us Adore Him E2011, 1979 | Nativity | RT | **$253** |
| Come Let Us Adore Him E2395 (Fish Mark), 1983 | Mini Nativity | OP | **$145** |
| Come Let Us Adore Him E2395 (Hourglass Mark), 1982 | Mini Nativity | OP | **$165** |
| Come Let Us Adore Him, set of 9, E2800, 1980 | Nativity | DS | **$300** |
| Come Let Us Adore Him E2810, 1980 | Musical Nativity | SU | **$160** |
| Come Let Us Adore Him E2810, 1984+ | Musical Nativity | SU | **$105** |
| Come Let Us Adore Him E2810 (Fish Mark), 1983 | Musical Nativity | SU | **$130** |
| Come Let Us Adore Him E2810 (Hourglass Mark), 1982 | Musical Nativity | SU | **$135** |
| Come Let Us Adore Him E2810 (Triangle Mark), 1981 | Musical Nativity | SU | **$140** |
| Come Let Us Adore Him E5619, 1984+ | Nativity | SU | **$30** |
| Come Let Us Adore Him E5619 (Fish Mark), 1983 | Nativity | SU | **$35** |

| Title | Series | Limit | Trend |
|---|---|---|---|
| Come Let Us Adore Him E5619 (Hourglass Mark), 1982 | Nativity | SU | **$35** |
| Come Let Us Adore Him E5619 (No Mark), 1980 | Nativity | SU | **$60** |
| Come Let Us Adore Him E5619 (Triangle Mark), 1981 | Nativity | SU | **$45** |
| Come Let Us Adore Him/Mini Nativity Starter Set 142743, 1995 | Mini Nativity | OP | **$30** |
| Come Let Us Adore Him Nativity Starter Set 142735, 1995 | Nativity | OP | **$44** |
| Companionship Happens In Our Club 635286, 2000 | Collectors' Club | CL | **$60** |
| Conductor Sam 150169, 1995 | Sugar Town | YR | **$22** |
| Confirmed In the Lord 488178, 1999 | General Line | OP | **$27** |
| Congratulations, Princess 106208, 1986 | General Line | RT | **$50** |
| Congratulations, You Earned Your Stripes 127809, 1995 | Noah's Ark/ Two By Two | RT | **$19** |
| Cosmos Ambitious, October 101526, 2002 | Calendar Girl | OP | **$36** |
| Count Each Birthday With a Joyful Smile 630018, 2007 | General Line | OP | **$40** |

| Title | Series | Limit | Trend |
|---|---|---|---|
| Count Your Blessings 4001646, 2005 | General Line | * | **$45** |
| Count Your Many Blessings 879274, 2001 | Show Exclusive | CL | **$50** |
| Couple On Stump, A 770744, 2000 | General Line | CL | **$25** |
| Courteous Service 791113, 2002 | Girls Festival | OP | **$60** |
| Cow With Bell Figurine E5638, 1981 | Nativity | RT | **$45** |
| Cross Walk 649511, 2001 | Little Moments Signs of Guidance | OP | **$20** |
| Crown Him King of Kings (Camel) 118263, 2004 | Nativity | OP | **$30** |
| Crown Him King of Kings (Cow) 118264, 2004 | Nativity | OP | **$30** |
| Crown Him King of Kings (Horse) 118262, 2004 | Nativity | OP | **$30** |
| Crown Him Lord of All E2803, 1980-1981 | Nativity | SU | **$110** |
| Crown Him Lord of All E2803 (Cross Mark), 1984 | Nativity | SU | **$80** |
| Crown Him Lord of All E2803 (Fish Mark), 1983 | Nativity | SU | **$80** |

| Title | Series | Limit | Trend |
|---|---|---|---|
| Crown Him Lord of All E2803 (Hourglass Mark), 1982 | Nativity | SU | **$90** |
| Crown Him Lord of All E2807, 1980 | Musical | SU | **$135** |
| Crown Him Lord of All E2807 (Cross Mark), 1984 | Musical | SU | **$100** |
| Crown Him Lord of All E2807 (Fish Mark), 1983 | Musical | SU | **$115** |
| Crown Him Lord of All E2807 (Hourglass Mark), 1982 | Musical | SU | **$120** |
| Crown Him Lord of All E2807 (Triangle Mark), 1981 | Musical | SU | **$125** |
| Curved Sidewalk 533149, 1994 | Sugar Town | RT | **$14** |
| Daddy's Little Angel (Blonde) 887951, 2002 | General Line | OP | **$25** |
| Daddy's Little Angel (Brunette) 887935, 2002 | General Line | OP | **$25** |
| Daddy's Little Girl 891045, 2002 | Family | SU | **$36** |
| Daisy Wide-Eyed & Innocent, July 101522, 2002 | Calendar Girl | OP | **$36** |
| Dance of the Lion 791121, 2001 | Century Circle | RT | **$90** |
| Dance to Your Own Beat 117799, 2004 | Special Wishes | OP | **$28** |

Daddy's Little Angel, Brunette 887935, 2002, **$25.**

Dawn's Early Light PM831, Precious Moments Collectors' Club, 1983, **$40.**

| Title | Series | Limit | Trend |
|---|---|---|---|
| Daniel and the Lion's Den 488291, 1998 | Little Moments Bible Stories | OP | **$20** |
| David and Goliath 650064, 2001 | General Line | OP | **$20** |
| Dawn's Early Light PM831, 1983 | Collectors' Club | CL | **$40** |
| Days Till Christmas 119217, 2004 | General Line | * | **$25** |
| Dear Friend, My Love For You Will Never Fade Away 114018, 2004 | General Line | OP | **$54** |
| Dear Jon, I Will Never Leave You—Jesus 588091, 1999 | Country Lane | RT | **$50** |
| December 110116, 1988 | Calendar Girl | RT | **$35** |
| December 261327, 1996 | Little Moments Birthstone Collection | OP | **$20** |
| December Girl With Waterball 844403, 2001 | General Line | * | **$18** |
| Dedicated to God 488232, 2000 | General Line | OP | **$32** |

Diamond—Color of Purity box 335576, Birthstone series, 1997, **$25.**

| Title | Series | Limit | Trend |
|---|---|---|---|
| Delivering Good News to You 488135, 2003 | Collectors' Club | * | **$N/A** |
| Dew Remember Me 101555, 2002 | Syndicated Exclusive | 5000 | **$40** |
| Diamond—Color of Purity, April 335576, 1998 | Birthstone | OP | **$25** |
| Different Beats Can Still Come Together 791148, 2001 | Japanese Exclusive | OP | **$55** |
| Do Not Open Till Christmas 522244, 1992 | Musical | SU | **$87** |
| Do This In Memory of Me (Boy) 640023, 2007 | General Line | OP | **$40** |
| Do This In Memory of Me (Girl) 640022, 2007 | General Line | OP | **$40** |
| Doctor's Office Nightlight 529869, 1994 | Sugar Town | RT | **$60** |
| Doctor's Office Set 529281, 1994 | Sugar Town | YR | **$238** |
| Dog and Kitten On Park Bench 529540, 1995 | Sugar Town | RT | **$17** |
| Dog E9267B, | Animal Collection | SU | **$15** |
| Donkey Figurine E5621, 1980 | Nativity | RT | **$25** |

| Title | Series | Limit | Trend |
|---|---|---|---|
| Donkey, Camel, Cow 279323, 1997 | Mini Nativity | SU | **$55** |
| Don't Fret, We'll Get You There Yet F0102, 2000 | Fun Club | CL | **$7** |
| Don't Let the Holidays Get You Down 522112, 1988 | General Line | RT | **$55** |
| Don't Rome Too Far From Home (Italy) 456403, 1998 | Little Moments International | OP | **$23** |
| Double Tree 533181, 1994 | Sugar Town | RT | **$18** |
| Dr. Sam Sugar 529850, 1994 | Sugar Town | RT | **$16** |
| Dream Is a Wish Your Heart Makes, A 620031, | Disney Showcase Collection | OP | **$65** |
| Dreams Bloom With a Seed of Faith 114031, 2003 | General Line | 7500 | **$36** |
| Dreams Really Do Come True 128309, 1994 | Special Wishes | SU | **$35** |
| Dreams Really Do Come True 640041, 2007 | General Line | OP | **$65** |
| Dropping In For Christmas E2350, 1982 | General Line | SU | **$44** |
| Dropping In For the Holidays 531952, 1994 | General Line | RT | **$65** |

Dreams Really Do Come True 128309, 1994, **$35.**

| Title | Series | Limit | Trend |
|-------|--------|-------|-------|
| Dropping Over For Christmas E2375, 1984+ | General Line | RT | **$65** |
| Dropping Over For Christmas E2375 (Fish Mark), 1983 | General Line | RT | **$70** |
| Dropping Over For Christmas E2375 (Hourglass Mark), 1982 | General Line | RT | **$110** |
| Dusty 529176, 1993 | Sammy's Circus | SU | **$24** |
| Dusty 529435, 1992 | Sugar Town | RT | **$16** |
| Each Hour Is Precious With You 163791, 1996 | To Have & to Hold | OP | **$65** |
| Easter's On Its Way 521892, 1989 | General Line | RT | **$62** |
| Easy As ABC 620023, 2006 | Picture Perfect Moments | OP | **$20** |
| Eat Ham 587842, 1999 | Country Lane | SU | **$22** |
| Eat Turkey 763225, 2000 | Country Lane | SU | **$25** |
| Eggs Over Easy E3118, 1980 | General Line | RT | **$120** |
| Eggs Over Easy E3118 (Fish Mark), 1983 | General Line | RT | **$60** |
| Eggs Over Easy E3118 (Hourglass Mark), 1982 | General Line | RT | **$75** |
| Eggs Over Easy E3118 (Triangle Mark), 1981 | General Line | RT | **$100** |

Eggs Over Easy E3118, 1980, **$60-$120.**

Egg-Specially For You
520667, 1988, **$45.**

The End is in
Sight E9253,
1982, **$55-$100.**

| Title | Series | Limit | Trend |
|---|---|---|---|
| Egg-Specially For You 520667, 1988 | General Line | RT | **$45** |
| Egg-Specially For You 550005, 2006 | General Line | OP | **$45** |
| El Senor Es La Esperanza De Nuestro Futuro 889563, 2000 | General Line | SU | **$40** |
| Elephants 530131, 1993 | Noah's Ark/ Two By Two | RT | **$22** |
| Embraced In Your Love 630041, 2007 | General Line | 3000 | **$100** |
| Emerald—Color of Patience, May 335584, 1998 | Birthstone | OP | **$25** |
| Enchantment Angel 634948, 1999 | General Line | * | **$20** |
| End Is In Sight, The E9253, 1984+ | General Line | SU | **$55** |
| End Is In Sight, The E9253 (Fish Mark), 1983 | General Line | SU | **$75** |
| End Is In Sight, The E9253 (Hourglass Mark), 1982 | General Line | SU | **$80** |
| End Is In Sight, The E9253 (No Mark), 1982 | General Line | SU | **$100** |
| Enter His Court With Thanksgiving 521221, 1996 | General Line | RT | **$24** |

| Title | Series | Limit | Trend |
|-------|--------|-------|-------|
| Especially For Ewe E9282, 1984+ | General Line | SU | **$30** |
| Especially For Ewe E9282 (Fish Mark), 1983 | General Line | SU | **$30** |
| Especially For Ewe E9282 (Hourglass Mark), 1982 | General Line | SU | **$35** |
| Especially For Ewe E9282C (No Mark), 1988 | General Line | SU | **$45** |
| Even the Heavens Shall Praise Him 150312, 1998 | General Line | RT | **$131** |
| Event For All Seasons, An 530158, 1993 | Events | SU | **$38** |
| Event Worth Wading For, An 527319, 1992 | Events | CL | **$47** |
| Evergreen Tree 528684, 1992 | Sugar Town | RT | **$31** |
| Every Man's House Is His Castle BC921, 1991 | Birthday Club | CL | **$20** |
| Every Precious Moment Needs a Smile 111757, 2003 | Chapel Exclusive | OP | **$35** |
| Everybody Has a Part 731625, 2000 | Special Wishes | CL | **$50** |
| Everyday Hero 112857, 2003 | Special Wishes | OP | **$30** |

Enter His Court With Thanksgiving 521221, 1996, **$24.**

| Title | Series | Limit | Trend |
|---|---|---|---|
| Everything Is Beautiful In Its Own Way 730149, 2001 | General Line | SU | **$30** |
| Everything's Better When Shared Together 108597, 2003 | Endangered Species | 7500 | **$45** |
| Everything's Better With a Friend 4004158, 2006 | Disney Showcase Collection | OP | **$60** |
| Ewe Are So Precious to Me 892726, 2001 | General Line | SU | **$40** |
| Ewe Are So Special to Me BC991, 1999 | Fun Club | CL | **$24** |
| Express Who You Are and You'll Be a Star 116611, 2004 | General Line | CL | **$35** |
| Faith Is Heaven's Sweet Song 975893, 2002 | Easter Seals Heaven's Grace | OP | **$125** |
| Faith Is the Victory 283592, 1997 | Collectors' Club | CL | **$75** |
| Faith Is the Victory 521396 (Bow & Arrow Mark), 1989 | General Line | RT | **$165** |
| Faith Is the Victory 521396 (Flame Mark), 1990 | General Line | RT | **$115** |
| Faith Takes the Plunge 111155, 1988 | General Line | SU | **$51** |

| Title | Series | Limit | Trend |
|---|---|---|---|
| Faith Takes the Plunge 111155 (Smiling), 1988 | General Line | SU | **$60** |
| Faithful Follower 4024086, 2005 | General Line | OP | **$40** |
| Fall Festival 732494, 2000 | General Line | OP | **$150** |
| Family Cat 848832, 2001 | Little Moments Build a Family | OP | **$10** |
| Family Dog 848824, 2001 | Little Moments Build a Family | OP | **$10** |
| Family of Love, A 0000366, 2004 | Gcc Exclusive | LE | **$45** |
| Family's Fur-Ever 108526, 2003 | General Line | OP | **$32** |
| February 109991, 1988 | Calendar Girl | RT | **$27** |
| February 261246, 1996 | Little Moments Birthstone Collection | OP | **$20** |
| February Girl With Waterball 844284, 2001 | General Line | * | **$18** |
| Feed My Sheep PM871, 1987 | Collectors' Club | CL | **$35** |

Faith Takes the Plunge 111155, smiling version, 1988, **$60.**

| Title | Series | Limit | Trend |
|---|---|---|---|
| Feliz Navidad (Boy) 610020, 2006 | General Line | OP | **$30** |
| Feliz Navidad (Girl) 610019, 2006 | General Line | OP | **$30** |
| Fence 529796, 1992 | Sugar Town | RT | **$14** |
| Festival of Precious Moments, A 270741, 270741B, 270741C, 1997 | Regional Conference | YR | **$66** |
| Fifteen Years Tweet Music Together Plaque 529087, 1993 | General Line | YR | **$48** |
| Filled With Wonder and Awe In the Holy Spirit 640021, 2007 | General Line | OP | **$35** |
| Find Your Wings and Fly 4001025, 2005 | General Line | OP | **$35** |
| Fire Hydrant 150215, 1995 | Sugar Town | RT | **$7** |
| First Noel, The E2365, 1982 | Nativity | SU | **$56** |
| First Noel, The E2366, 1982 | Nativity | SU | **$56** |
| Fishing For Friends BC861, 1986 | Birthday Club | CL | **$102** |
| Flag Pole With Kitten 184136, 1996 | Sugar Town | RT | **$12** |

| Title | Series | Limit | Trend |
|-------|--------|-------|-------|
| Flight Into Egypt 455970, 1998 | General Line | CL | **$80** |
| Flower Girl E2835, 1984 | Bridal Party | OP | **$17** |
| Flowers and Friendship Are Best When Shared 630011, 2007 | General Line | OP | **$50** |
| Focusing In On Those Precious Moments C0018, 1998 | Collectors' Club | CL | **$24** |
| Focusing In On Those Precious Moments C0118, 1998 | Collectors' Club | CL | **$28** |
| Follow Your Heart 528080, 1995 | Events | YR | **$37** |
| Follow Your Heart 640042, 2007 | General Line | OP | **$65** |
| For An Angel You're So Down to Earth 283444, 1997 | Mini Nativity | SU | **$18** |
| For God So Loved the World E5382, 1984 | Nativity | SU | **$107** |
| For His Precious Love First Communion Boy 0000365, 2004 | General Line | OP | **$24** |
| For His Precious Love First Communion Girl 0000364, 2004 | General Line | OP | **$24** |

Fishing for Friends BC861, Precious Moments Birthday Club,
1986, **$102.**

| Title | Series | Limit | Trend |
|---|---|---|---|
| For the Sweetest Tu-Lips In Town (Brunette) 306959B, 2002 | General Line | OP | **$35** |
| For the Sweetest Tu-Lips In Town 306959, 1998 | General Line | OP | **$26** |
| Forever In Our Hearts 108541, 2003 | Special Wishes | OP | **$28** |
| Forever True Couple Musical 537926, 1999 | General Line | OP | **$60** |
| Forgiving Is Forgetting E9252, 1981 | General Line | SU | **$64** |
| Fork Over Those Blessings 307033, 1998 | Country Lane | RT | **$40** |
| Four Seasons, The, set of 4 thimbles, 100641, 1986 | General Line | CL | **$87** |
| Free Christmas Puppies 528064, 1994 | Sugar Town | RT | **$21** |
| Friday's Child Is Loving and Giving 692123, 2001 | Days of the Week | OP | **$20** |
| Friend Is Someone Who Cares, A 520632, 1988 | General Line | RT | **$74** |
| Friend Like You Is Heaven-Scent, A 523607, 2006 | General Line | OP | **$45** |
| Friends Always Deserve Special Treatment 108538, 2003 | General Line | OP | **$45** |

| Title | Series | Limit | Trend |
|-------|--------|-------|-------|
| Friends Are Forever, Sew Bee It 455903, 1998 | General Line | RT | **$56** |
| Friends Are Never Far Behind 101543, 2002 | Smiles Forever | 5000 | **$45** |
| Friends From the Very Beginning 261068, 1997 | General Line | RT | **$38** |
| Friends Let You Be You 116612, 2004 | Precious Moments Rocks Tour | OP | **$30** |
| Friends Make Life More Fun 114918, 2003 | Boys & Girls Clubs of America | RT | **$80** |
| Friends Never Drift Apart 100250, 1985 | General Line | RT | **$68** |
| Friends of a Feather Shop Together 114019, 2004 | General Line | OP | **$50** |
| Friends Share a Special Bond 104219, 2002 | General Line | OP | **$40** |
| Friends to the End 104418, 1988 | Birthday Series | SU | **$16** |
| Friends to the Very End 526150, 1993 | General Line | RT | **$39** |
| Friends Write From the Start C0021, 2001 | Collectors' Club | * | **$29** |
| Friends Write From the Start C0121, 2001 | Collectors' Club | * | **$25** |

For the Sweetest Tu-Lips in Town 306959B, 2002, **$35.**

Friday's Child is Loving and Giving 692123, Days of the Week series, 2001, **$20.**

The Four Seasons series: Winter's Song, **$119**; Autumn's Praise, **$50**; Summer's Joy, **$89**; and The Voice of Spring, **$140.**

| Title | Series | Limit | Trend |
|---|---|---|---|
| Friendship Angel 682365, 1999 | General Line | OP | **$34** |
| Friendship Grows When You Plant a Seed 524271, 1990 | General Line | RT | **$40** |
| Friendship Hits the Spot 306916, 1997 | Baby Classics | OP | **$59** |
| Friendship Hits the Spot 520748, 1988 | General Line | RT | **$64** |
| Friendship Is a Sweet Journey 720012, 2007 | General Line | OP | **$50** |
| Friendship Is a Sweet Journey waterball 721001, 2007 | General Line | OP | **$25** |
| Friendship's a Slice of Life 634964, 2000 | General Line | OP | **$35** |
| From Small Beginnings Come Great Things (1970s) 4001671, 2005 | Through the Years | 7500 | **$32** |
| From the First Time I Spotted You I Knew We'd Be Friends 260940, 1997 | Birthday Series | RT | **$23** |
| From This Day Forward 550027, 2006 | General Line | OP | **$75** |
| Fruit of the Spirit Is Love, Joy and Peace, The 710017, 2007 | General Line | OP | **$50** |

Friends Never Drift Apart 100250, 1985, **$68.**

| Title | Series | Limit | Trend |
|-------|--------|-------|-------|
| Fruit of the Spirit Is Love, The 521213, 1992 | General Line | RT | **$23** |
| Fuel Boy Donny 531871, 1995 | Sugar Town | RT | **$26** |
| Fun Is Being Together, The 730262, 2000 | Century Circle | CL | **$200** |
| Fun Starts Here, The B0012, 1997 | Birthday Club | CL | **$22** |
| Fun Starts Here, The B0112, 1997 | Birthday Club | CL | **$23** |
| Future Is In Our Hands, The 730068, 2000 | General Line | CL | **$31** |
| Galloping Toward Tomorrow 958859, 2002 | General Line | RT | **$115** |
| Garbage Can 272914, 1997 | Sugar Town | RT | **$26** |
| Garnet—Color of Boldness, January 335533, 1998 | Birthstone | OP | **$25** |
| Gather Your Dreams 529680, 1993 | Easter Seals | CL | **$565** |
| Get Into the Habit of Prayer 12203, 1984 | General Line | SU | **$49** |

| Title | Series | Limit | Trend |
|-------|--------|-------|-------|
| Get Your Kicks on Route 66, 2007 | Events | 1,000 | **$55** |
| Gift Is In the Giving, The 710010, 2007 | General Line | OP | **$50** |
| Giraffes 530115, 1993 | Noah's Ark/ Two By Two | RT | **$19** |
| Girl Angel Messenger of Love 119838, 2004 | General Line | OP | **$20** |
| Girls Rule 115919, 2004 | Special Wishes | OP | **$35** |
| Girls With Gifts 531812, 1995 | Sugar Town | RT | **$29** |
| Give a Grin and Let the Fun Begin 488011, 2000 | Birthday Train | OP | **$23** |
| Give Ability a Chance 192368, 1997 | Easter Seals | SU | **$34** |
| Give 'Em a Brake For Jesus 649562, 2001 | Little Moments Signs of Guidance | OP | **$20** |
| Give With a Grateful Heart 0000382, 2004 | General Line | OP | **$24** |
| Give Your Whole Heart 490245, 2000 | Easter Seals | CL | **$28** |
| Giving My Heart Freely 650013, 2000 | General Line | SU | **$30** |

From Small Beginnings Come Great Things 4001671, Through the Years series, 2005, **$32.**

Get Into the Habit of Prayer 12203, 1984, **$49.**

| Title | Series | Limit | Trend |
|-------|--------|-------|-------|
| Glad We See Eye to Eye 113991, 2003 | Special Wishes | OP | **$25** |
| Go 4 It 649538, 1999 | Little Moments Signs of Guidance | OP | **$20** |
| Goat Figurine E2364, 1982 | Nativity | SU | **$55** |
| God Bless America 102938, 1985 | America Forever | LE | **$39** |
| God Bless America 102938R, 2002 | America Forever | OP | **$36** |
| God Bless Our Family 100498, 1986 | General Line | RT | **$53** |
| God Bless Our Family 100501, 1986 | General Line | RT | **$53** |
| God Bless Our Home 12319, 1985 | General Line | RT | **$77** |
| God Bless Our Home BC941, 1994 | Birthday Club | CL | **$27** |
| God Bless Our Years Together 12440, 1985 | Collectors' Club | CL | **$265** |
| God Bless the Bride E2832, 1984 | General Line | SU | **$50** |
| God Bless the Day We Found You 100145, 1985 | General Line | SU | **$72** |

| Title | Series | Limit | Trend |
|---|---|---|---|
| God Bless the Day We Found You 100145R, 1995 | General Line | RT | **$65** |
| God Bless the Day We Found You 100153, 1985 | General Line | SU | **$55** |
| God Bless the Day We Found You 100153R, 1995 | General Line | RT | **$42** |
| God Bless the U.S.A. 527564, 1992 | General Line | LE | **$27** |
| God Bless You For Touching My Life PM881, 1988 | Collectors' Club | CL | **$47** |
| God Bless You Graduate 106194, 1986 | General Line | OP | **$30** |
| God Bless You On Your Birthday 15962, 1985 | Birthday Train | OP | **$16** |
| God Bless You With Bouquets of Victory 283584, 1997 | Collectors' Club | CL | **$31** |
| God Bless You With Rainbows nightlight 16020, 1986 | General Line | SU | **$100** |
| God Blessed Our Year Together E2854, 1983 | Anniversary Figurines | RT | **$61** |
| God Blessed Our Years Together With So Much Love and Happiness E2853, 1984 | Anniversary Figurines | OP | **$73** |
| God Blessed Our Years Together With So Much Love and Happiness E2854, 1984 | General Line | OP | **$72** |

God Bless America 102938, America Forever series, 1985, **$39.**

God Bless Our Home 12319, 1985, **$77.**

God Bless Our Years Together 12440, 1985, **$265.**

| Title | Series | Limit | Trend |
|---|---|---|---|
| God Blessed Our Years Together With So Much Love and Happiness E2855, 1984 | Anniversary Figurines | SU | **$77** |
| God Blessed Our Years Together With So Much Love and Happiness E2856, 1984 | Anniversary Figurines | SU | **$77** |
| God Blessed Our Years Together With So Much Love and Happiness E2857, 1984 | Anniversary Figurines | RT | **$60** |
| God Blessed Our Years Together With So Much Love and Happiness E2859, 1984 | Anniversary Figurines | SU | **$74** |
| God Blessed Our Years Together With So Much Love and Happiness E2860, 1984 | Anniversary Figurines | RT | **$64** |
| God Cared Enough to Send His Best 524476, 1994 | General Line | RT | **$75** |
| God Gave His Best 15806, 1985 | Family Christmas | SU | **$10** |
| God Gives Us Memories So That We Might Have Roses In December 680990, 2000 | General Line | RT | **$45** |
| God Has Sent His Son E0507, 1983 | General Line | SU | **$93** |
| God Is Love E5213, 1980 | General Line | SU | **$120** |
| God Is Love E5213, 1984+ | General Line | SU | **$55** |

God Bless the U.S.A. 527564, 1992, **$27.**

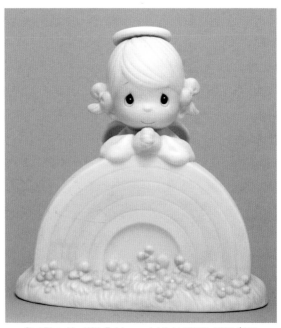

God Bless You With Rainbows nightlight 16020, 1986, **$100.**

God Blessed Our Year Together With So Much Love and Happiness
E2854, Anniversary series, 1984, **$61.**

God Gave His Best 15806, Family Christmas Scene, 1985, **$10.**

God is Love E5213, 1980, **$55-$120.**

God is Love,
Dear Valentine
thimble
100625,
1986, **$15.**

God is Love, Dear Valentine
523518, 1989, **$20.**

| Title | Series | Limit | Trend |
|---|---|---|---|
| God Is Love E5213 (Fish Mark), 1983 | General Line | SU | **$75** |
| God Is Love E5213 (Hourglass Mark), 1982 | General Line | SU | **$80** |
| God Is Love E5213 (Triangle Mark), 1981 | General Line | SU | **$85** |
| God Is Love, Dear Valentine 523518, 1989 | General Line | RT | **$20** |
| God Is Love, Dear Valentine E7153, 1984+ | General Line | SU | **$30** |
| God Is Love, Dear Valentine E7153 (Fish Mark), 1983 | General Line | SU | **$35** |
| God Is Love, Dear Valentine E7153 (Hourglass Mark), 1982 | General Line | SU | **$40** |
| God Is Love, Dear Valentine E7153 (Triangle Mark), 1981 | General Line | SU | **$45** |
| God Is Love, Dear Valentine E7154, 1984+ | General Line | SU | **$30** |
| God Is Love, Dear Valentine E7154 (Fish Mark), 1983 | General Line | SU | **$35** |
| God Is Love, Dear Valentine E7154 (Hourglass Mark), 1982 | General Line | SU | **$40** |

| Title | Series | Limit | Trend |
|---|---|---|---|
| God Is Love, Dear Valentine E7154 (Triangle Mark), 1981 | General Line | SU | **$45** |
| God Is Love, Dear Valentine thimble 100625, 1986 | General Line | SU | **$15** |
| God Is Watching Over You E7163, 1981 | General Line | SU | **$79** |
| God Knows Our Ups and Downs 490318, 2000 | General Line | RT | **$35** |
| God Loves a Happy Camper 587893, 2000 | General Line | OP | **$36** |
| God Loveth a Cheerful Giver 272477, 1997 | Baby Classics | RT | **$24** |
| God Loveth a Cheerful Giver E1378, 1979 | General Line | RT | **$798** |
| God Rest Ye Merry Gentlemen 112878, 2003 | Christmas Remembered | RT | **$55** |
| God Sends the Gift of His Love E6613, 1984 | General Line | SU | **$34** |
| God Sent His Love 15881, 1985 | Christmas Annual | CL | **$23** |
| God Sent His Love thimble 15865, 1985 | General Line | YR | **$38** |
| God Sent You Just In Time 15504, 1985 | Musical | RT | **$55** |
| God Shed His Grace On Thee 106632, 2002 | General Line | CL | **$60** |

God Loveth a Cheerful Giver E1378, 1979, one of the Original 21 figurines, **$798.**

| Title | Series | Limit | Trend |
|---|---|---|---|
| God Understands E1379B, 1979 | General Line | SU | **$122** |
| God Understands E1379B, 1980 | General Line | SU | **$120** |
| God Understands E1379B (Cross Mark), 1984 | General Line | SU | **$80** |
| God Understands E1379B (Fish Mark), 1983 | General Line | SU | **$85** |
| God Understands E1379B (Hourglass Mark), 1982 | General Line | SU | **$85** |
| God Understands E1379B (Triangle Mark), 1981 | General Line | SU | **$90** |
| Godchild Close to My Heart, A (Baby) 804096, 2001 | General Line | OP | **$25** |
| Godchild Close to My Heart, A (Boy) 811815, 2001 | General Line | SU | **$32** |
| Godchild Close to My Heart, A (Girl) 811807, 2001 | General Line | OP | **$35** |
| Godmother & Me (Boy) 115904, 2004 | General Line | OP | **$25** |
| Godmother & Me (Girl) 115905, 2004 | General Line | OP | **$25** |
| God's Children At Play 649481, 1999 | Little Moments Signs of Guidance | OP | **$16** |
| God's Love Has No Measure 890871, 2002 | General Line | OP | **$25** |

| Title | Series | Limit | Trend |
|---|---|---|---|
| God's Love Is Crystal Clear 879436, 2001 | Century Circle | CL | **$45** |
| God's Love Is Reflected In You 175277, 1996 | Century Circle | 1,500 | **$199** |
| God's Love Is Reflected In You 175277S, 1996 | General Line | CL | **$600** |
| God's Promises Are Sure E9260, 1984+ | Heavenly Halos | SU | **$55** |
| God's Promises Are Sure E9260 (Fish Mark), 1983 | Heavenly Halos | SU | **$65** |
| God's Promises Are Sure E9260 (Fish Stamp), 1983 | Heavenly Halos | SU | **$95** |
| God's Ray of Mercy PM841, 1983 | Collectors' Club | CL | **$42** |
| God's Speed E3112, 1980 | General Line | RT | **$105** |
| God's Speed E3112, 1983+ | General Line | RT | **$50** |
| God's Speed E3112 (Hourglass Mark), 1982 | General Line | RT | **$55** |
| God's Speed E3112 (Triangle Mark), 1981 | General Line | RT | **$75** |
| God's Speed PM992, 1999 | Collectors' Club | CL | **$30** |
| Going Home 525979, 1991 | General Line | OP | **$68** |
| Good Advice Has No Price 679828, 2000 | General Line | OP | **$30** |
| Good Fortune Dragon 731633, 2000 | General Line | CL | **$30** |

| Title | Series | Limit | Trend |
|---|---|---|---|
| Good Friends Are For Always 524123, 1991 | General Line | RT | **$27** |
| Good Friends Are Forever 272422, 1996 | Baby Classics | RT | **$27** |
| Good Friends Are Forever 521817, 1989 | General Line | RT | **$34** |
| Good Friends Are Forever 525049, 1990 | Events | 200 | **$760** |
| Good Lord Always Delivers (Brunette), The 523453B, 2001 | General Line | SU | **$30** |
| Good Lord Always Delivers, The 523453, 1990 | General Line | SU | **$38** |
| Good Lord Has Blessed Us Tenfold, The 114022, 1987 | General Line | LE | **$191** |
| Good Lord Will Always Up-hold Us, The 325325, 1998 | General Line | RT | **$56** |
| Good News Is So Uplifting 523615, 1990 | General Line | RT | **$60** |
| Good Samaritan, The 649988, 1999 | Little Moments Bible Stories | OP | **$25** |
| Grandfather 529516, 1992 | Sugar Town | RT | **$29** |
| Grandma & Me (Boy) 115902, 2004 | General Line | OP | **$25** |

God's Speed E3112, 1980, **$50-$105.**

Good
Friends Are
For Always
524123,
1991, **$27.**

The Good Lord
Always Delivers
523453, 1990, **$38.**

Grandma's Prayer PM861, Precious Moments Collectors' Club, 1986, **$58.**

| Title | Series | Limit | Trend |
|-------|--------|-------|-------|
| Grandma & Me (Girl) 115903, 2004 | General Line | OP | **$25** |
| Grandma, I'll Never Outgrow You (Boy) 731595, 2000 | General Line | OP | **$25** |
| Grandma, I'll Never Outgrow You (Girl) 798223, 2000 | General Line | CL | **$45** |
| Grandma, I'll Never Outgrow You 731587, 2000 | General Line | SU | **$25** |
| Grandma's Little Angel (Blonde Boy) 887978, 2002 | General Line | OP | **$25** |
| Grandma's Little Angel (Blonde Girl) 887900, 2001 | General Line | OP | **$25** |
| Grandma's Little Angel (Brunette Boy) 887986, 2002 | General Line | OP | **$39** |
| Grandma's Little Angel (Brunette Girl) 887927, 2002 | General Line | OP | **$38** |
| Grandma's Love Is One Size Fits All, A, 117801, 2004 | General Line | OP | **$32** |
| Grandma's Prayer PM861, 1986 | Collectors' Club | CL | **$58** |
| Gratitude With Attitude 730041, 2001 | General Line | OP | **$32** |
| Great Pearl, The 649996, 1999 | Little Moments Bible Stories | OP | **$20** |

| Title | Series | Limit | Trend |
|---|---|---|---|
| Greatest Gift Is a Friend, The 109231, 1987 | General Line | RT | **$40** |
| Greatest of These Is Love, The 521868, 1988 | General Line | SU | **$38** |
| Groom (African-American) 795372, 2001 | General Line | OP | **$30** |
| Groom (Asian) 795410, 2001 | General Line | OP | **$30** |
| Groom (Caucasian Brunette ) 874493, 2001 | Lord Bless You and Keep You | SU | **$50** |
| Groom (Hispanic) 795399, 2000 | General Line | SU | **$30** |
| Groom E2837, 1986 | Bridal Party | OP | **$27** |
| Grounds For a Great Friendship 108536, 2003 | General Line | OP | **$45** |
| Growing In Wisdom (Boy) 481645, 1998 | Special Wishes | CL | **$25** |
| Growing In Wisdom (Girl) 481653, 1998 | Special Wishes | CL | **$25** |
| Growing Love, A E0008, 1988 | Collectors' Club | CL | **$32** |
| Growing Love, A E0108, 1988 | Collectors' Club | CL | **$40** |

The Greatest Gift is a Friend 109231, 1987, **$40.**

A Growing Love E0108, Precious Moments Collectors' Club, 1988, **$40.**

Happiness is the Lord 12378, Rejoice in the Lord series, 1985, **$32.**

| Title | Series | Limit | Trend |
|---|---|---|---|
| Guide Us to Thy Perfect Light 610017, 2006 | General Line | CL | **$35** |
| Hail Mary, Full of Grace 635006, 2003 | General Line | OP | **$72** |
| Hallelujah Country 105821, 1987 | General Line | RT | **$50** |
| Hallelujah For the Cross 532002, 1995 | General Line | RT | **$24** |
| Hallelujah Hoedown 163864, 1996 | Events | SU | **$31** |
| Halo and Merry Christmas 12351, 1985 | General Line | SU | **$145** |
| Hand That Rocks the Future E3108, 1980 | General Line | SU | **$90** |
| Hand That Rocks the Future E3108 (Cross Mark), 1984 | General Line | SU | **$60** |
| Hand That Rocks the Future E3108 (Fish Mark), 1983 | General Line | SU | **$60** |
| Hand That Rocks the Future E3108 (Hourglass Mark), 1982 | General Line | SU | **$65** |
| Hand That Rocks the Future E3108 (Title Error, No Mark), 1980 | General Line | SU | **$195** |
| Hand That Rocks the Future E3108 (Triangle Mark), 1981 | General Line | SU | **$70** |

| Title | Series | Limit | Trend |
|---|---|---|---|
| Hand That Rocks the Future E5204, 1980 | Musical | RT | **$105** |
| Hand That Rocks the Future E5204, 1983+ | Musical | RT | **$80** |
| Hand That Rocks the Future E5204 (Hourglass Mark), 1982 | Musical | RT | **$85** |
| Hand That Rocks the Future E5204 (Triangle Mark), 1981 | Musical | RT | **$90** |
| Hang On to That Holiday Feeling 455962, 1998 | Mini Nativity | RT | **$25** |
| Hank and Sharon 184098, 1996 | Sugar Town | RT | **$30** |
| Happily Ever After 550029, 2006 | General Line | OP | **$55** |
| Happiness Divine 109584, 1987 | General Line | RT | **$42** |
| Happiness Is a Song From Heaven 112969, 2004 | Heaven's Grace | RT | **$112** |
| Happiness Is At Our Fingertips 529931, 1992 | General Line | CL | **$40** |
| Happiness Is Being a Mom 115926, 2006 | General Line | OP | **$50** |
| Happiness Is Being a Mom waterball 551004, 2006 | General Line | CL | **$25** |

| Title | Series | Limit | Trend |
|---|---|---|---|
| Happiness Is Belonging B0008, 1994 | Birthday Club | CL | **$18** |
| Happiness Is Belonging B0108, 1994 | Birthday Club | CL | **$22** |
| Happiness Is the Lord 12378, 1985 | Rejoice In the Lord | SU | **$32** |
| Happiness to the Core 261378, 1997 | Catalog Exclusive | SU | **$36** |
| Happy Anniversary 804444, 2003 | 25th Anniversary | LE | **$35** |
| Happy Birdie 527343, 1992 | Birthday Series | SU | **$14** |
| Happy Birthday 163686, 1998 | General Line | DS · | **$35** |
| Happy Birthday Dear Jesus 524875, 1989 | Nativity | SU | **$16** |
| Happy Birthday Jesus 272523, 1997 | General Line | OP | **$30** |
| Happy Birthday Jesus 530492, 1993 | Mini Nativity | RT | **$15** |
| Happy Birthday Little Lamb 15946, 1985 | Birthday Train | OP | **$15** |
| Happy Birthday Poppy 106836, 1987 | General Line | SU | **$33** |
| Happy Birthday to Ewe 531561, 1999 | General Line | OP | **$32** |

| Title | Series | Limit | Trend |
|---|---|---|---|
| Happy Birthday to Our Love 114021, 2003 | General Line | OP | **$45** |
| Happy Days Are Here Again 104396, 1986 | General Line | SU | **$36** |
| Happy Hula Days 128694, 1995 | General Line | OP | **$30** |
| Happy Trails PM981, 1998 | Collectors' Club | CL | **$53** |
| Happy Trip 521280, 1989 | General Line | SU | **$32** |
| Hare's to the Birthday Club BC971, 1997 | Birthday Club | CL | **$23** |
| Hark the Harold Angel Sings 104211, 2002 | Nativity | OP | **$20** |
| Have a Beary Merry Christmas 522856, 1989 | Family Christmas | SU | **$18** |
| Have a Beary Special Birthday B0004, 1989 | Birthday Club | CL | **$23** |
| Have a Beary Special Birthday B0104, 1989 | Birthday Club | CL | **$29** |
| Have a Cozy Country Christmas 455873, 1998 | General Line | OP | **$44** |
| Have a Heavenly Journey 12416R, 1998 | General Line | RT | **$21** |
| Have Faith In God 505153, 2000 | Victorian Series | RT | **$47** |

Happy Birthday, Little Lamb
15946, Birthday Train, 1985, **$15.**

Have a Beary Special Birthday
B0104, Precious Moments
Birthday Club, 1989, **$29.**

Have a Cozy
Country
Christmas
455873, 1998,
**$44.**

| Title | Series | Limit | Trend |
|---|---|---|---|
| Have I Got News For You 105635, 1986 | Nativity | SU | **$48** |
| Have I Got News For You 528137, 1994 | Mini Nativity | RT | **$19** |
| Have I Toad You Lately That I Love You 521329, 1996 | General Line | CL | **$44** |
| Have You Any Room For Jesus 261130, 1997 | General Line | RT | **$48** |
| Have You Herd How Much I Love You? 108593, 2003 | Endangered Species | 7,500 | **$45** |
| Have Your Cake and Eat It Too 550028, 2006 | General Line | OP | **$50** |
| Have Your Cake Cake Topper 634022, 2007 | General Line | OP | **$25** |
| Have Your Cake musical water-globe 631003, 2007 | General Line | OP | **$25** |
| Having a Sister Is Always Having a Friend 640031, 2007 | General Line | OP | **$50** |
| Hawthorne Bright and Hopeful, May 101520, 2002 | Calendar Girl | OP | **$40** |
| Hay Good Lookin' 649732, 2000 | Country Lane | RT | **$38** |
| He Came As the Gift of God's Love 528129, 1999 | Mini Nativity | OP | **$30** |
| He Careth For You E1377B, 1979 | Nativity | SU | **$135** |

| Title | Series | Limit | Trend |
|---|---|---|---|
| He Careth For You E1377B, 1980 | Nativity | SU | **$155** |
| He Careth For You E1377B (Cross Mark), 1984 | Nativity | SU | **$90** |
| He Careth For You E1377B (Fish Mark), 1983 | Nativity | SU | **$95** |
| He Careth For You E1377B (Hourglass Mark), 1982 | Nativity | SU | **$105** |
| He Careth For You E1377B (Triangle Mark), 1981 | Nativity | SU | **$110** |
| He Cleansed My Soul 100277, 1986 | General Line | OP | **$55** |
| He Cleansed My Soul 306940, 1998 | Baby Classics | OP | **$25** |
| He Covers the Earth With His Beauty 142654, 1995 | Christmas Annual | SU | **$40** |
| He Covers the Earth With His Glory (Winter) 129135, 1999 | Four Seasons | RT | **$44** |
| He Graces the Earth With Abundance (Fall) 129119, 1999 | Four Seasons | RT | **$44** |
| He Is My Guiding Light 550021, 2006 | Chapel Exclusive | OP | **$50** |
| He Is My Inspiration 523038, 1990 | Chapel Exclusive | OP | **$84** |

| Title | Series | Limit | Trend |
|---|---|---|---|
| He Is My Salvation 135984, 2000 | General Line | RT | **$40** |
| He Is My Song 12394, 1984 | Rejoice In the Lord | SU | **$28** |
| He Is Not Here For He Is Risen As He Said 527106, 1993 | Chapel Exclusive | OP | **$59** |
| He Is Our Shelter From the Storm 523550, 1997 | Boys & Girls Clubs of America | RT | **$56** |
| He Is the Star of the Morning 522252, 1988 | General Line | SU | **$68** |
| He Leadeth Me E1377A, 1979 | Nativity | SU | **$145** |
| He Leadeth Me E1377A, 1980 | Nativity | SU | **$124** |
| He Leadeth Me E1377A (Cross Mark), 1984 | Nativity | SU | **$90** |
| He Leadeth Me E1377A (Fish Mark), 1983 | Nativity | SU | **$90** |
| He Leadeth Me E1377A (Hourglass Mark), 1982 | Nativity | SU | **$95** |
| He Leadeth Me E1377A (Triangle Mark), 1981 | Nativity | SU | **$105** |
| He Leadeth Me E1377R, 1998 | Nativity | YR | **$12** |
| He Leads Me Beside the Still Waters 523305, 1997 | Chapel Exclusive | 7,500 | **$50** |

| Title | Series | Limit | Trend |
|---|---|---|---|
| He Loves Me 152277, 1996 | Easter Seals | CL | **$550** |
| He Loves Me 524263, 1991 | General Line | CL | **$31** |
| He Restoreth My Soul 523364, 1998 | Chapel Exclusive | 7,500 | **$55** |
| He Shall Cover You With His Wings 306835, 1998 | Dated Cross | YR | **$38** |
| He Shall Lead the Children Into the 21st Century 127930, 1999 | General Line | CL | **$225** |
| He Upholdeth Those Who Fall E0526, 1984-1985 | General Line | SU | **$115** |
| He Upholdeth Those Who Fall E0526 (Fish Mark), 1983 | General Line | SU | **$95** |
| He Walks With Me 107999, 1987 | Easter Seals | CL | **$37** |
| He Watches Over Us All E3105, 1980 | General Line | SU | **$70** |
| He Watches Over Us All E3105 (Cross Mark), 1984 | General Line | SU | **$50** |
| He Watches Over Us All E3105 (Fish Mark), 1983 | General Line | SU | **$55** |
| He Watches Over Us All E3105 (Hourglass Mark), 1982 | General Line | SU | **$55** |
| He Watches Over Us All E3105 (Triangle Mark), 1981 | General Line | SU | **$60** |

Hawthorn "Bright and Hopeful," May 101520, Calendar Girl series, 2002, **$40.**

He Cleansed My Soul 100277, 1986, **$55.**

He is My Song 12394, Rejoice in the Lord series, 1984, **$28.**

He Leadeth Me E1377R,
Navitity series, 1998, **$12.**

He Walks With Me 107999,
Easter Seals, 1987, **$37.**

He Watches Over Us All
E3105, 1980, **$50-$70.**

He's the Healer of Broken Hearts
100080, 1987, **$49.**

Heaven Bless You 520934, 1990, **$78.**

| Title | Series | Limit | Trend |
|---|---|---|---|
| He Watches Over Us All PM993, 1999 | Collectors' Club | CL | **$225** |
| Head and Shoulders Above the Rest 108598, 2003 | Endangered Species | 7,500 | **$45** |
| Healing Begins With Forgiveness 892157, 2002 | Family | SU | **$42** |
| Heart of a Mother Is Reflected In Her Child, The (Boy) 640001, 2007 | General Line | OP | **$30** |
| Heart of a Mother Is Reflected In Her Child, The (Girl) 640002, 2007 | General Line | OP | **$30** |
| Heather 272833, 1997 | Sugar Town | RT | **$26** |
| Heaven Bless You 100285, 1984 | Musical | SU | **$69** |
| Heaven Bless You 456314, 1999 | Easter Seals | CL | **$33** |
| Heaven Bless You 520934, 1990 | General Line | RT | **$78** |
| Heaven Bless Your Special Day 15954, 1985 | Birthday Train | OP | **$16** |
| Heaven Bless Your Togetherness 106755, 1986 | General Line | RT | **$84** |
| Heaven Must Have Sent You 521388, 1998 | General Line | RT | **$59** |

| Title | Series | Limit | Trend |
|-------|--------|-------|-------|
| Heaven Sent 4004374, 2005 | General Line | OP | **$38** |
| Heavenly Daze-Dream Makers 879630, 2004 | Heavenly Daze | RT | **$77** |
| Heavenly Daze-Golden Town Seamstress 879606, 2002 | Heavenly Daze | RT | **$85** |
| Heavenly Daze-Halo Maker 879576, 2002 | Heavenly Daze | RT | **$85** |
| Heavenly Daze-Star Smith Vignette 879568, 2001 | Heavenly Daze | RT | **$85** |
| Heavenly Daze-The Good Book Library 879622, 2003 | Heavenly Daze | RT | **$85** |
| Heavenly Light E5637, 1983+ | Nativity | RT | **$35-$40** |
| Heavenly Light E5637 (Hourglass Mark), 1982 | Nativity | RT | **$60** |
| Heavenly Light E5637 (Triangle Mark), 1981 | Nativity | RT | **$65** |
| Heigh Ho, It's off to Play We Go 630038, 2006 | Disney Showcase Collection | OP | **$65** |
| He'll Carry Me Through 488089, 2000 | General Line | RT | **$36** |
| Hello World! 521175, 1988 | Birthday Series | RT | **$12** |

| Title | Series | Limit | Trend |
|---|---|---|---|
| Hello, Lord, It's Me Again PM811 (Hourglass Mark), 1982 | Collectors' Club | CL | **$375** |
| Hello, Lord, It's Me Again PM811 (Triangle Mark), 1981 | Collectors' Club | CL | **$385** |
| Help, Lord, I'm In a Spot 100269, 1985 | General Line | RT | **$61** |
| Her Children Will Rise Up and Call Her Blessed 550025, 2006 | General Line | YR | **$90** |
| He's Got the Whole World In His Hands 526886, 1995 | Easter Seals | CL | **$550** |
| He's the Healer of Broken Hearts 100080, 1987 | General Line | RT | **$49** |
| Hi Sugar BC871, 1987 | Birthday Club | CL | **$50** |
| High Hopes 521957, 1990 | General Line | SU | **$29** |
| Highway to Happiness 649457, 2001 | Little Moments Signs of Guidance | OP | **$16** |
| His Blessings Are Without Measure 113966, 2003 | General Line | RT | **$36** |
| His Burden Is Light Covered Box 488429, 1998 | General Line | OP | **$25** |
| His Burden Is Light E1380G, 1979 | General Line | RT | **$160** |

Heaven Must Have Sent You 521388, 1998, **$59.**

The Heavenly Light E5637,
Nativity series, 1981, **$35-$65.**

High Hopes 521957,
1990, **$29.**

| Title | Series | Limit | Trend |
|---|---|---|---|
| His Burden Is Light E1380G, 1980 | General Line | RT | **$155** |
| His Burden Is Light E1380G (Cross Mark), 1984 | General Line | RT | **$85** |
| His Burden Is Light E1380G (Fish Mark), 1983 | General Line | RT | **$95** |
| His Burden Is Light E1380G (Hourglass Mark), 1982 | General Line | RT | **$105** |
| His Burden Is Light E1380G (Triangle Mark), 1981 | General Line | RT | **$120** |
| His Eye Is On the Sparrow E0530, 1987 | General Line | RT | **$64** |
| His Hope Lights My Way 4024085, 2005 | General Line | OP | **$50** |
| His Little Treasure PM931, 1993 | Collectors' Club | CL | **$34** |
| His Love Is Reflected In You 104279, 2003 | General Line | OP | **$77** |
| His Love Will Shine On You 522376, 1989 | Easter Seals | YR | **$29** |
| His Love Will Uphold the World 539309, 1999 | General Line | SU | **$146** |
| His Name Is Jesus E5381, 1984 | Nativity | SU | **$89** |

| Title | Series | Limit | Trend |
|---|---|---|---|
| His Presence Is Felt In the Chapel 163872, 1996 | Chapel Exclusive | RT | **$38** |
| His Sheep Am I E7161 (Cross Mark), 1984 | Nativity | SU | **$60** |
| His Sheep Am I E7161 (Fish Mark), 1983 | Nativity | SU | **$65** |
| His Sheep Am I E7161 (Hourglass Mark), 1982 | Nativity | SU | **$70** |
| His Truth Is Marching On 4003178, 2005 | General Line | OP | **$20** |
| Hisssterrically Sweet 821969, 2001 | Japanese Exclusive | OP | **$16** |
| Hogs and Kisses 261106, 1998 | Country Lane | OP | **$48** |
| Hogs and Kisses 261106S, 1998 | Country Lane | 1,500 | **$170** |
| Hola Amigo (Mexico) 456454, 1998 | Little Moments International | OP | **$35** |
| Hold On to the Moment FC003, 2000 | Fun Club | CL | **$7** |
| Hold On to Your Faith (Boy) 113947, 2004 | General Line | OP | **$32** |
| Hold On to Your Faith (Girl) 113946, 2004 | General Line | OP | **$32** |
| Holiday Surprises Come In All Sizes 488348, 2004 | General Line | OP | **$30** |

His Burden is Light E1380G, 1979, one of the Original 21 figurines, **$85-$160.**

His Sheep Am I E7161, Nativity series, 1982, **$60-$70.**

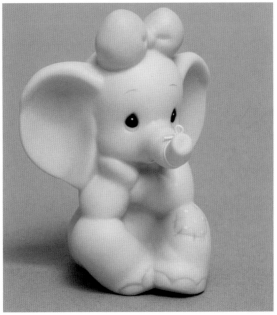

How Can I Ever Forget You 526924, Birthday series, 1991, **$15.**

| Title | Series | Limit | Trend |
|---|---|---|---|
| Holiday Wishes Sweetie Pie 312444, 1997 | Little Moments | OP | **$24** |
| Holly Full of Foresight, December 101528, 2002 | Calendar Girl | OP | **$36** |
| Holy Mackerel, It's Your Birthday 994898, 2003 | Animal Affections | OP | **$20** |
| Holy Smokes E2351, 1984+ | General Line | RT | **$85** |
| Holy Smokes E2351 (Fish Mark), 1983 | General Line | RT | **$105** |
| Holy Smokes E2351 (Hourglass Mark), 1982 | General Line | RT | **$130** |
| Holy Tweet BC972, 1997 | Birthday Club | CL | **$28** |
| Home Is Where the Heart Is 325481, 2000 | Catalog Exclusive | SU | **$42** |
| Home Made of Love 730211, 2000 | General Line | RT | **$40** |
| Honk If You Love Jesus 15490, 1985 | Nativity | RT | **$20** |
| Hope Blooms In a Garden of Glory 114027, 2003 | General Line | 7,500 | **$36** |
| Hope Is a Gentle Melody 112967, 2004 | Heaven's Grace | OP | **$125** |
| Hope Is Revealed Through God's Word 488259, 1998 | Victorian Series | YR | **$27** |

| Title | Series | Limit | Trend |
|---|---|---|---|
| Hope You're Over the Hump 521671, 1993 | Birthday Series | SU | **$24** |
| Hope You're Up and On the Trail Again 521205, 1990 | General Line | SU | **$43** |
| Hopping For the Best (1950s) 4001670, 2005 | Through the Years | 7,500 | **$45** |
| Hoppy Birthday B0010, 1995 | Birthday Club | CL | **$20** |
| Hoppy Birthday B0110, 1995 | Birthday Club | CL | **$24** |
| Hoppy Easter, Friend 521906, 1990 | General Line | RT | **$41** |
| How Can I Ever Forget You 526924, 1991 | Birthday Series | RT | **$15** |
| How Can Three Work Together Except They Agree PM983, 1998 | Collectors' Club | CL | **$133** |
| How Can Two Work Together Except They Agree E9263, 1983 | General Line | SU | **$175** |
| How Do You Spell Mom with frame 115907, 2004 | General Line | RT | **$25** |
| How Sweet It Is to Be Loved By You 630001, 2007 | General Line | OP | **$50** |
| Hug One Another 521299, 1990 | General Line | RT | **$42** |

How Can Two Work Together Except They Agree E9263, 1983, **$175** .

| Title | Series | Limit | Trend |
|---|---|---|---|
| Hugs Can Tame the Wildest Hearts 104282, 2002 | Events | CL | **$35** |
| Humble Prayers Make Hearts Bloom 114029, 2003 | General Line | 7,500 | **$45** |
| I Always Knew You'd Turn'ip 550017, 2006 | General Line | OP | **$25** |
| I Am a Bee-liever 928534, 2001 | Special Wishes | SU | **$30** |
| I Am Me! 120118, 2004 | Special Wishes | OP | **$30** |
| I Believe In Miracles 272469, 1997 | Baby Classics | RT | **$17** |
| I Believe In Miracles E7156, 1984-1985 | General Line | SU | **$50** |
| I Believe In Miracles E7156 (Fish Mark), 1983 | General Line | SU | **$70** |
| I Believe In Miracles E7156 (Hourglass Mark), 1982 | General Line | SU | **$75** |
| I Believe In Miracles E7156R (Bluebird Version), 1987 | General Line | RT | **$170** |
| I Believe In the Old Rugged Cross 103632, 1985 | General Line | RT | **$37** |
| I Belong to the Lord 520853, 1988 | General Line | SU | **$33** |

I Believe in Miracles E7156, 1982, **$50-$75.**

| Title | Series | Limit | Trend |
|-------|--------|-------|-------|
| I Can't Bear to Let You Go 532037, 1995 | General Line | RT | **$36** |
| I Can't Give You Anything But Love 112864, 2003 | Special Wishes | OP | **$27** |
| I Can't Spell Success Without You 523763, 1990 | General Line | SU | **$39** |
| I Couldn't Make It Without You 635030, 1999 | Boys & Girls Clubs of America | CL | **$60** |
| I Found My Love In You 630027, 2007 | Bluebirds of Happiness | OP | **$40** |
| I Get a Bang Out of You 12262, 1985 | Clown | RT | **$42** |
| I Get a Cluck Out of You 104270, 2002 | Country Lane | RT | **$36** |
| I Get a Kick Out of You E2827, 1984 | General Line | SU | **$185** |
| I Give You My Heart 0000974, 2005 | General Line | OP | **$32** |
| I Give You My Love Forever True 129100, 1994 | General Line | OP | **$65** |
| I Give You My Love Forever True 876143, 2001 | General Line | LE | **$150** |
| I Haven't Seen Much of You Lately 531057, 1996 | Birthday Series | RT | **$17** |

I Can't Bear to Let You Go 532037, 1995, **$36.**

I Get a Bang Out of You 12262, 1985, **$42.**

I Get a Kick Out of You E2827, 1984, **$185.**

| Title | Series | Limit | Trend |
|---|---|---|---|
| I Hope You're Up and On the Trail Again 521205, 1989 | General Line | SU | **$60** |
| I Just Go Bats Over You 110260, 2003 | Animal Affections | OP | **$20** |
| I Love Thee With An Everlasting Love 620011, 2006 | General Line | OP | **$55** |
| I Love to Tell the Story PM852, 1985 | Collectors' Club | CL | **$59** |
| I Love You a Bushel and a Peck 110265, 2003 | Animal Affections | OP | **$20** |

| Title | Series | Limit | Trend |
|---|---|---|---|
| I Love You a Bushel and a Peck E1541, 2003 | General Line | OP | **$20** |
| I Love You Forever and Always 113944, 2004 | General Line | YR | **$65** |
| I Love You Knight and Day 108604, 2003 | General Line | OP | **$40** |
| I Love You More Every Day 114032, 2004 | General Line | OP | **$32** |
| I Love You This Much (Boy) 4001673, 2005 | General Line | OP | **$27** |
| I Love You This Much (Girl) 4001668, 2005 | General Line | OP | **$30** |
| I M the One You Love 4004372, 2005 | General Line | OP | **$25** |
| I Now Pronounce You Man and Wife 455938, 1998 | General Line | OP | **$27** |
| I Only Have Arms For You 527769, 1992 | Birthday Series | RT | **$16** |
| I Only Have Ice For You 530956, 1995 | General Line | RT | **$55** |
| I Picked a Very Special Mom 100536, 1986 | General Line | CL | **$48** |
| I Picked You to Love (Boy) 4001811, 2005 | General Line | OP | **$27** |

I Love to Tell the Story PM852, Precious Moments Collectors' Club, 1985, **$59.**

I Only Have Ice for You 530956, 1995, **$55.**

| Title | Series | Limit | Trend |
|-------|--------|-------|-------|
| I Picked You to Love (Girl) 4001810, 2005 | General Line | OP | **$30** |
| I Pray the Lord My Soul to Keep 632341, 2003 | Little Moments | OP | **$28** |
| I Pray the Lord My Soul to Keep 632430, 2003 | Little Moments | OP | **$28** |
| I Saw Mommy Kissing Santa Claus 455822, 1998 | General Line | SU | **$57** |
| I See Bright Hope In the Future 973912, 2002 | Events | CL | **$45** |
| I Still Do 530999, 1993 | Anniversary Figurines | OP | **$27** |
| I Still Do 531006, 1993 | Anniversary Figurines | OP | **$30** |
| I Think You're Just Divine 272558, 1997 | General Line | RT | **$26** |
| I Trust In the Lord For My Strength 104798, 2002 | General Line | OP | **$25** |
| I Will Always Be Thinking of You 523631, 1994 | General Line | RT | **$48** |
| I Will Always Care For You 550041, 2006 | General Line | OP | **$45** |
| I Will Always Love You 523569, 2001 | General Line | CL | **$45** |

I Pray the Lord My Soul to Keep 632430, Little Moments, 2003, **$28.**

I Will Always Be Thinking of You 523631, 1994, **$48.**

I Will Love You All Ways 679704, 1999, **$225.**

| Title | Series | Limit | Trend |
|---|---|---|---|
| I Will Cherish the Old Rugged Cross 523534, 1990 | General Line | CL | **$28** |
| I Will Fear No Evil 523356, 1998 | Chapel Exclusive | 7,500 | **$43** |
| I Will Love You All Ways 679704, 1999 | General Line | RT | **$225** |
| I Will Make You Fishers of Men 522139, 2003 | General Line | LE | **$44** |
| I Will Never Leaf You 114958, 2005 | General Line | OP | **$30** |
| I Would Be Lost Without You 526142, 1990 | General Line | RT | **$20** |
| I Would Be Sunk Without You 102970, 1986 | General Line | RT | **$16** |
| Ice See a Champion In You 649937, 1999 | General Line | CL | **$80** |
| Ice Skating Pond Precious Skape 750131, 2000 | General Line | OP | **$36** |
| Icy Good Times Ahead 112839, 2003 | General Line | YR | **$35** |
| I'd Be Lost Without You 108592, 2003 | Endangered Species | 7,500 | **$45** |
| I'd Go Anywhere With You 120117, 2004 | General Line | RT | **$30** |

| Title | Series | Limit | Trend |
|-------|--------|-------|-------|
| I'd Goat Anywhere With You 163694, 1996 | Noah's Ark/ Two By Two | RT | **$16** |
| I'd Jump Through Hoops For You 104799, 2002 | Special Wishes | OP | **$23** |
| I'd Travel the Highlands to Be With You (Scotland) 456470, 1998 | Little Moments International | OP | **$35** |
| If God Be For Us, Who Can Be Against Us E9285 (Cross Mark), 1984 | General Line | SU | **$75** |
| If God Be For Us, Who Can Be Against Us E9285 (Fish Mark), 1983 | General Line | SU | **$90** |
| If the Shoe Fits, Buy It! 114010, 2003 | Special Wishes | OP | **$36** |
| If You Could Only See Heaven 111753, 2003 | Chapel Exclusive | OP | **$45** |
| I'll Be Your Shelter In the Storm 550003, 2006 | General Line | OP | **$35** |
| I'll Give Him My Heart 150088, 1995 | General Line | RT | **$33** |
| I'll Give You the World Box 798290, 2000 | General Line | CL | **$25** |
| I'll Never Let You Down 730165, 2001 | General Line | OP | **$45** |

| Title | Series | Limit | Trend |
|---|---|---|---|
| I'll Never Stop Loving You 521418, 1989 | General Line | RT | **$50** |
| I'll Never Stop Loving You 649465, 2001 | Little Moments Signs of Guidance | OP | **$16** |
| I'll Never Tire of You 307068, 1998 | Country Lane | RT | **$90** |
| I'll Play My Drum For Him E2355, 1982 | Musical | SU | **$160** |
| I'll Play My Drum For Him E2356, 1982 | Nativity | SU | **$68** |
| I'll Play My Drum For Him E2360, 1983+ | Nativity | RT | **$28-$40** |
| I'll Play My Drum For Him E2360 (Hourglass Mark), 1982 | Nativity | RT | **$45** |
| I'll Play My Drum For Him E5384, 1984 | Mini Nativity | RT | **$30** |
| I'll Weight For You 521469, 2000 | Catalog Exclusive | CL | **$29** |
| I'm a Big Brother 101503, 2001 | General Line | SU | **$20** |
| I'm a Big Sister 101502, 2001 | General Line | SU | **$20** |
| I'm a Fool For You 4004737, 2005 | General Line | OP | **$35** |

I Will Never Leaf You
114958, 2005, **$30.**

I'd Go Anywhere With You
120117, 2004, **$30.**

I'll Never Let You Down
730165, 2001, **$45.**

I'm a Possibility 100188,
1986, **$40.**

I'm Following Jesus PM862, Precious Moments Collectors' Club, 1986, **$35.**

| Title | Series | Limit | Trend |
|---|---|---|---|
| I'm a Possibility 100188, 1986 | General Line | RT | **$40** |
| I'm a Precious Moments Fan 523526, 1990 | Events | CL | **$29** |
| I'm a Reflection of Your Love 730238, 2000 | Avon Exclusive | OP | **$15** |
| I'm a Sucker For Your Love 630003, 2007 | General Line | OP | **$35** |
| I'm Always Bee-Side You 4001661, 2005 | Easter Seals | RT | **$40** |
| I'm Completely Suspended With Love 526096, 2001 | Special Wishes | YR | **$23** |
| I'm Completely Suspended With Love 526096S, 2001 | Special Wishes | RT | **$25** |
| I'm Dreaming of a White Christmas 272590, 1997 | General Line | RT | **$35** |
| I'm Falling For Somebunny Box E9266B, 1988 | General Line | SU | **$50** |
| I'm Filled With Love For You 108548, 2003 | Sea of Friendship | OP | **$36** |
| I'm Following Jesus PM862, 1986 | Collectors' Club | CL | **$35** |
| I'm Gonna Stick With You 117797, 2004 | General Line | RT | **$36** |
| I'm Nuts Over My Collection BC902, 1990 | Birthday Club | CL | **$26** |

| Title | Series | Limit | Trend |
|-------|--------|-------|-------|
| I'm Proud to Be An American-Air Force (Boy) 588156, 2000 | General Line | OP | **$35** |
| I'm Proud to Be An American-Air Force (Boy) 730033, 2000 | General Line | SU | **$35** |
| I'm Proud to Be An American-Air Force (Girl) 729914, 2000 | General Line | OP | **$35** |
| I'm Proud to Be An American-Air Force (Girl) 729965, 2000 | General Line | OP | **$35** |
| I'm Proud to Be An American-Army (Boy) 588105, 2000 | General Line | OP | **$58** |
| I'm Proud to Be An American-Army (Girl) 729876, 2000 | General Line | OP | **$35** |
| I'm Proud to Be An American-Army (Girl) 729922, 2000 | General Line | OP | **$35** |
| I'm Proud to Be An American-Coast Guard (Boy) 588148, 2000 | General Line | OP | **$35** |
| I'm Proud to Be An American-Coast Guard (Boy) 730025, 2000 | General Line | OP | **$35** |
| I'm Proud to Be An American-Coast Guard (Girl) 729906, 2000 | General Line | OP | **$35** |

| Title | Series | Limit | Trend |
|---|---|---|---|
| I'm Proud to Be An American-Coast Guard (Girl) 729957, 2000 | General Line | OP | **$35** |
| I'm Proud to Be An American-Marine (Boy) 588113, 2000 | General Line | OP | **$58** |
| I'm Proud to Be An American-Marine (Boy) 730009, 2000 | General Line | OP | **$58** |
| I'm Proud to Be An American-Marine (Girl) 729884, 2000 | General Line | OP | **$35** |
| I'm Proud to Be An American-Marine (Girl) 729930, 2000 | General Line | SU | **$35** |
| I'm Proud to Be An American-Navy (Boy) 588121, 2000 | General Line | OP | **$35** |
| I'm Proud to Be An American-Navy (Boy) 730017, 2000 | General Line | OP | **$35** |
| I'm Proud to Be An American-Navy (Girl) 729892, 2000 | General Line | OP | **$35** |
| I'm Proud to Be An American-Navy (Girl) 729949, 2000 | General Line | OP | **$35** |
| I'm Sending You a Merry Christmas 455601, 1998 | Christmas Annual | CL | **$31** |
| I'm Sending You a White Christmas 112402, 1987 | Musical | RT | **$95** |
| I'm Sending You a White Christmas E2829, 1984 | General Line | RT | **$78** |

I'm Gonna
Stick With You
117797, 2004,
**$36.**

I'm So Glad
God Has
Blessed
Me With a
Friend Like
You 523623,
1992, **$58.**

I'm Proud to Be An American-Marine Boy 588113, 2000, **$58.**

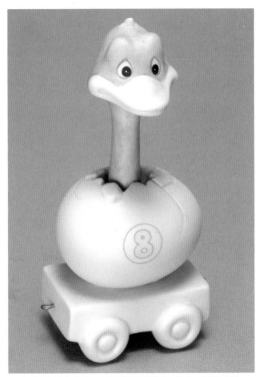

Isn't Eight Just Great 109460, Birthday Train, 1988, **$23.**

Isn't He Precious E5379, Nativity series, 1984, **$36.**

It Is Better to Give Than to Receive 12297, 1985, **$42.**

| Title | Series | Limit | Trend |
|---|---|---|---|
| I'm So Glad God Blessed Me With a Friend Like You 523623, 1992 | General Line | RT | **$58** |
| I'm So Glad I Spotted You As a Friend 108539, 2003 | General Line | OP | **$23** |
| I'm So Glad You Fluttered Into My Life 520640, 1989-1991 | General Line | RT | **$308** |
| I'm So Glad You Fluttered Into My Life 520640 (Flower Mark), 1988 | General Line | RT | **$345** |
| I'm So Lucky to Have You As a Daughter 104269, 2002 | General Line | OP | **$32** |
| I'm Sorry 114011, 2003 | Special Wishes | OP | **$27** |
| I'm There For You Rain Or Shine 118361, 2004 | General Line | OP | **$30** |
| Immersed In God's Love 4004680, 2005 | General Line | OP | **$40** |
| In All Things Give Thanks 610068, 2006 | General Line | OP | **$45** |
| In God's Beautiful Garden of Love 261629, 1997 | Century Circle | 15,000 | **$107** |
| In His Time PM872, 1987 | Collectors' Club | CL | **$29** |

| Title | Series | Limit | Trend |
|---|---|---|---|
| In the Spotlight of His Grace 520543, 1990 | General Line | SU | **$30** |
| Infant Angel, 1995 | Growing In Grace | OP | **$27** |
| I-rish You Lots of Luck 108535, 2003 | Special Wishes | OP | **$27** |
| Isn't Eight Just Great 109460, 1988 | Birthday Train | OP | **$23** |
| Isn't He Precious 522988, 1988 | Mini Nativity | SU | **$29** |
| Isn't He Precious E5379, 1984 | Nativity | RT | **$36** |
| Isn't He Wonderful E5639 1984-1985 | Nativity | SU | **$40** |
| Isn't He Wonderful E5639 (Fish Mark), 1983 | Nativity | SU | **$50** |
| Isn't He Wonderful E5639 (Hourglass Mark), 1982 | Nativity | SU | **$50** |
| Isn't He Wonderful E5639 (Triangle Mark), 1981 | Nativity | SU | **$75** |
| Isn't He Wonderful E5640, 1984-1985 | Nativity | SU | **$55** |
| Isn't He Wonderful E5640 (Fish Mark), 1983 | Nativity | SU | **$60** |
| Isn't He Wonderful E5640 (Hourglass Mark), 1982 | Nativity | SU | **$65** |

| Title | Series | Limit | Trend |
|-------|--------|-------|-------|
| Isn't He Wonderful E5640 (Triangle Mark), 1981 | Nativity | SU | **$65** |
| It Is Better to Give Than to Receive 12297, 1985 | General Line | SU | **$42** |
| It Is No Secret What God Can Do 531111, 1993 | General Line | LE | **$42** |
| It May Be Greener, But It's Just As Hard to Cut 163899, 1996 | General Line | RT | **$36** |
| It Only Takes a Moment to Show You Care CC790001, 2007 | Collectors' Club | * | **$32** |
| It's a Banner Day, Congratulations 795259, 2001 | Special Wishes | OP | **$23** |
| It's a Girl-Blonde 136204, 1995 | Growing In Grace | OP | **$25** |
| It's a Girl-Brunette 136204B, 2002 | Growing In Grace | OP | **$25** |
| It's a Perfect Boy 525286, 1990 | Mini-Nativity | RT | **$19** |
| It's a Perfect Boy E0512, 1983 | Nativity | SU | **$93** |
| It's Almost Time For Santa 532932, 2001 | General Line | CL | **$75** |
| It's Down Hill All the Way—Congratulations 110261, 2003 | Animal Affections | OP | **$18** |

It's a Girl-Blonde 136204, Growing in Grace series, 1995, **$25.**

It's Ruff to Always Be Cheery 272639, Little Moments, 1997, **$20.**

Jesus is Coming Soon 12343, 1985, **$29.**

| Title | Series | Limit | Trend |
|-------|--------|-------|-------|
| It's No Secret What God Can Do 531111, 1994 | Easter Seals | SU | **$42** |
| It's No Yolk When I Say I Love You 522104, 1990 | General Line | SU | **$85** |
| It's Only Gauze I Care 112862, 2003 | Special Wishes | OP | **$30** |
| It's Ruff to Always Be Cheery 272639, 1997 | Little Moments | OP | **$20** |
| It's So Uplifting to Have a Friend Like You 524905, 1992 | General Line | RT | **$30** |
| It's the Birthday of a King 102962, 1985 | Nativity | SU | **$29** |
| It's Time to Bless Your Own Day C0022, 2002 | Collectors' Club | * | **$25** |
| It's Time to Blow Your Own Horn 4001664, 2005 | General Line | OP | **$45** |
| It's What's Inside That Counts 101497, 2002 | General Line | OP | **$32** |
| It's What's Inside That Counts E3119, 1980 | General Line | SU | **$120** |
| It's What's Inside That Counts E3119 (Cross Mark), 1984 | General Line | SU | **$85** |
| It's What's Inside That Counts E3119 (Fish Mark), 1983 | General Line | SU | **$85** |

| Title | Series | Limit | Trend |
|---|---|---|---|
| It's What's Inside That Counts E3119 (Hourglass Mark), 1982 | General Line | SU | **$90** |
| It's What's Inside That Counts E3119 (Triangle Mark), 1981 | General Line | SU | **$110** |
| It's Your Birthday, Go Bananas 116946, 2004 | Birthday Train | OP | **$23** |
| It's Your Birthday, Live It Up 116945, 2004 | Birthday Train | OP | **$25** |
| I've Got a Crush On You 120122, 2004 | General Line | OP | **$27** |
| I've Got You Under My Skin BC922, 1992 | Birthday Club | CL | **$30** |
| Jan 529826, 1994 | Sugar Town | RT | **$24** |
| January 109983, 1988 | Calendar Girl | RT | **$30** |
| January 261203, 1996 | Little Moments Birthstone Collection | OP | **$20** |
| January Girl With Waterball 844276, 2001 | General Line | OP | **$30** |
| Jennifer 163708, 1996 | Sammy's Circus | SU | **$29** |

| Title | Series | Limit | Trend |
|---|---|---|---|
| Jest to Let You Know You're Tops B0006, 1991 | Birthday Club | CL | **$21** |
| Jest to Let You Know You're Tops B0106, 1991 | Birthday Club | CL | **$22** |
| Jesus Is Born 104210, 2002 | General Line | OP | **$40** |
| Jesus Is Born E2012, 1979 | Nativity | SU | **$103** |
| Jesus Is Born E2801, 1980 | Nativity | SU | **$355** |
| Jesus Is Born E2801 (Cross Mark), 1984 | Nativity | SU | **$300** |
| Jesus Is Born E2801 (Fish Mark), 1983 | Nativity | SU | **$290** |
| Jesus Is Born E2801 (Hourglass Mark), 1982 | Nativity | SU | **$295** |
| Jesus Is Born E2801 (Triangle Mark), 1981 | Nativity | SU | **$325** |
| Jesus Is Born E2809, 1980 | Musical | SU | **$140** |
| Jesus Is Born E2809 (Hourglass Mark), 1982 | Musical | SU | **$105** |
| Jesus Is Coming Soon 12343, 1985 | General Line | SU | **$29** |
| Jesus Is My Lighthouse 487945, 1999 | Show Exclusive | CL | **$75** |
| Jesus Is the Answer E1381, 1979 | General Line | SU | **$165** |

| Title | Series | Limit | Trend |
|---|---|---|---|
| Jesus Is the Answer E1381, 1980-1981 | General Line | SU | **$165** |
| Jesus Is the Answer E1381 (Cross Mark), 1984 | General Line | SU | **$115** |
| Jesus Is the Answer E1381 (Fish Mark), 1983 | General Line | SU | **$125** |
| Jesus Is the Answer E1381 (Hourglass Mark), 1982 | General Line | SU | **$130** |
| Jesus Is the Answer E1381R, 1992 | General Line | RT | **$58** |
| Jesus Is the Light E1373G, 1979 | General Line | RT | **$89** |
| Jesus Is the Light E1373G, 1980 | General Line | RT | **$100** |
| Jesus Is the Light E1373G, 1984-1988 | General Line | RT | **$40** |
| Jesus Is the Light E1373G (Fish Mark), 1983 | General Line | RT | **$40** |
| Jesus Is the Light E1373G (Hourglass Mark), 1982 | General Line | RT | **$50** |
| Jesus Is the Light E1373G (Triangle Mark), 1981 | General Line | RT | **$60** |
| Jesus Is the Light That Shines E0502, 1983 | General Line | SU | **$53** |
| Jesus Is the Only Way 520756, 1988 | General Line | SU | **$42** |

| Title | Series | Limit | Trend |
|---|---|---|---|
| Jesus Is the Sweetest Name I Know 523097, 1989 | Nativity | SU | **$36** |
| Jesus Loves Me (African-American Boy) 899771, 2001 | General Line | OP | **$33** |
| Jesus Loves Me (African-American Girl) 899879, 2001 | General Line | OP | **$20** |
| Jesus Loves Me (Asian-American Girl) 901555, 2001 | General Line | OP | **$33** |
| Jesus Loves Me (Latino Boy) 899526, 2001 | General Line | OP | **$20** |
| Jesus Loves Me 104531, 1988 | Easter Seals | CL | **$1240** |
| Jesus Loves Me 488380, 1998 | General Line | OP | **$45** |
| Jesus Loves Me 488399, 1998 | General Line | OP | **$25** |
| Jesus Loves Me 634735, 1999 | Easter Seals | CL | **$500** |
| Jesus Loves Me 745766, 2000 | General Line | CL | **N/A** |
| Jesus Loves Me E1372B, 1979 | General Line | RT | **$100** |
| Jesus Loves Me E1372B, 1980 | General Line | RT | **$81** |
| Jesus Loves Me E1372B, 1984 | General Line | RT | **$30** |
| Jesus Loves Me E1372B (Fish Mark), 1983 | General Line | RT | **$30** |
| Jesus Loves Me E1372B (Hourglass Mark), 1982 | General Line | RT | **$35** |

Jesus Loves Me E9278, 1983, **$35.**

Jesus Loves Me E1372B, 1979, **$30-$81.**

| Title | Series | Limit | Trend |
|---|---|---|---|
| Jesus Loves Me E1372B (Triangle Mark), 1981 | General Line | RT | **$55** |
| Jesus Loves Me E1372G, 1979 | General Line | RT | **$130** |
| Jesus Loves Me E1372G, 1980 | General Line | RT | **$125** |
| Jesus Loves Me E1372G, 1983+ | General Line | RT | **$45** |
| Jesus Loves Me E1372G (Hourglass Mark), 1982 | General Line | RT | **$50** |
| Jesus Loves Me E1372G (Triangle Mark), 1981 | General Line | RT | **$75** |
| Jesus Loves Me E9278, 1983+ | General Line | RT | **$20-35** |
| Jesus Loves Me E9278 (Hourglass Mark), 1982 | General Line | RT | **$35** |
| Jesus Loves Me E9279, 1984+ | General Line | RT | **$20** |
| Jesus Loves Me E9279 (Fish Mark), 1983 | General Line | RT | **$35** |
| Jesus Loves Me E9279 (Hourglass Mark), 1982 | General Line | RT | **$40** |
| Jesus Loves Me ES2000, 2000 | Easter Seals | CL | **$500** |
| Jesus Loves Me waterball 701068, 1999 | General Line | CL | **$25** |
| Jesus the Savior Is Born 520357, 1988 | Nativity | SU | **$51** |

Jesus Loves Me E1372G, 1979, one of the Original 21 figurines, **$45-$130.**

Jesus Loves Me E9279, 1982, **$20-$40.**

Join in On the Blessings E0404, Precious Moments Collectors' Club, 1984, **$29.**

| Title | Series | Limit | Trend |
|-------|--------|-------|-------|
| Join In On the Blessings E0104, 1984 | Collectors' Club | CL | **$39** |
| Join In On the Blessings E0404, 1984 | Collectors' Club | CL | **$29** |
| Jonah and the Whale 488283, 1998 | Little Moments Bible Stories | OP | **$23** |
| Jordan 529168, 1995 | Sammy's Circus | SU | **$26** |
| Joseph's Special Coat 488305, 1998 | Little Moments Bible Stories | OP | **$25** |
| Journey of Hope, A, 104277, 2004 | Special Wishes | OP | **$45** |
| Joy 610013, 2006 | General Line | OP | **$75** |
| Joy Is the Music of Angels 112966, 2003 | Easter Seals Heaven's Grace | OP | **$125** |
| Joy of the Lord Is My Strength, The 100137, 1986 | General Line | OP | **$48** |
| Joy On Arrival 523178, 1990 | General Line | SU | **$48** |
| Joy to the World E2344, 1982 | General Line | SU | **$92** |
| Joy to the World E5378, 1984 | Nativity | SU | **$60** |

| Title | Series | Limit | Trend |
|-------|--------|-------|-------|
| July 110051, 1988 | Calendar Girl | RT | **$55** |
| July 261289, 1996 | Little Moments Birthstone Collection | OP | **$20** |
| July Girl With Waterball 844330, 2001 | General Line | OP | **$30** |
| Jumping For Joy PM991, 1999 | Collectors' Club | CL | **$34** |
| June 110043, 1988 | Calendar Girl | RT | **$104** |
| June 261254, 1996 | Little Moments Birthstone Collection | OP | **$20** |
| June Girl With Waterball 844322, 2001 | General Line | OP | **$30** |
| Junior Bridesmaid E2845, 1983 | Bridal Party | OP | **$22** |
| Just a Happy Note 890960, 2002 | Special Wishes | OP | **$23** |
| Just a Line to Say You're Special 522864, 1995 | General Line | RT | **$36** |
| Just a Line to Wish You a Happy Day 520721, 1989 | General Line | SU | **$60** |

| Title | Series | Limit | Trend |
|---|---|---|---|
| Just a Little Paws For a Warm Welcome 120109, 2004 | Special Wishes | OP | **$25** |
| Just An Old Fashioned Hello 4004739, 2005 | Through the Years | 7,500 | **$45** |
| Just For Your Knowledge, I'll Miss Ya At College 108533, 2003 | Special Wishes | OP | **$36** |
| Just Poppin' In to Say Halo 523755, 1994 | General Line | RT | **$32** |
| Just the Facts, You're Terrific 320668, 1998 | Little Moments | OP | **$18** |
| Katie 529184, 1993 | Sammy's Circus | SU | **$18** |
| Katylynne 529524, 1992 | Sugar Town | RT | **$27** |
| Keep Looking Up 15997, 1985 | Birthday Train | OP | **$23** |
| Kind Hearts Send Showers of Love 620007, 2006 | General Line | OP | **$40** |
| Kindness of Spirit Knows No Bounds 114028, 2003 | General Line | OP | **$45** |
| Kindness of Spirit Knows No Bounds E1616, 2003 | General Line | 7,500 | **$36** |
| Kitten E9267D, 1988 | Animal Collection | SU | **$15** |

The Joy of the Lord is My Strength 100137, 1986, **$48.**

Just a Line to Wish You a Happy Day 520721, 1989, **$60.**

June 110043, Calendar Girl series, 1988, **$104.**

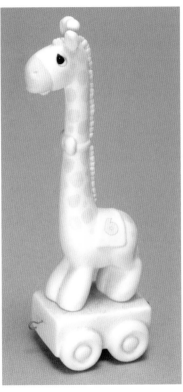

Keep Looking Up
15997, Birthday Train,
1985, **$23.**

| Title | Series | Limit | Trend |
|---|---|---|---|
| La Quinceanera 115871, 2003 | Special Wishes | OP | **$40** |
| Lamb E9267E, | Animal Collection | SU | **$15** |
| Lamp Post 529559, 1994 | Sugar Town | RT | **$13** |
| Lead Me to Calvary 260916, 1997 | Dated Cross | YR | **$25** |
| Leon & Evelyn Mae 529818, 1994 | Sugar Town | RT | **$23** |
| Leroy 184071, 1996 | Sugar Town | RT | **$28** |
| Let Freedom Ring 681059, 1999 | Special Wishes | OP | **$78** |
| Let Freedom Ring 681059E, 1999 | Special Wishes | RT | **$45** |
| Let Heaven and Nature Sing E2346, 1984-1989 | Musical | SU | **$105** |
| Let Heaven and Nature Sing E2346 (Fish Mark), 1983 | Musical | SU | **$130** |
| Let Heaven and Nature Sing E2346 (Hourglass Mark), 1982 | Musical | SU | **$145** |
| Let Him Enter Your Heart 649554, 2001 | Little Moments Signs of Guidance | OP | **$20** |

Let Love Reign E9273, 1982, **$105-$245.**

Let Us Call the Club to Order E0303, 1982, **$45-$50.**

Let's Keep in Touch musical 102520, 1986, **$84.**

| Title | Series | Limit | Trend |
|---|---|---|---|
| Let Love Reign 890596, 2002 | General Line | CL | **$60** |
| Let Love Reign E9273, 1984-1987 | General Line | RT | **$105** |
| Let Love Reign E9273 (Fish Mark), 1983 | General Line | RT | **$105** |
| Let Love Reign E9273 (Hourglass Mark), 1982 | General Line | RT | **$245** |
| Let Not the Sun Go Down Upon Your Wrath E5203, 1980 | General Line | SU | **$160** |
| Let Not the Sun Go Down Upon Your Wrath E5203 (Cross Mark), 1984 | General Line | SU | **$110** |
| Let Not the Sun Go Down Upon Your Wrath E5203 (Fish Mark), 1983 | General Line | SU | **$125** |
| Let Not the Sun Go Down Upon Your Wrath E5203 (Hourglass Mark), 1982 | General Line | SU | **$130** |
| Let Not the Sun Go Down Upon Your Wrath E5203 (Triangle Mark), 1981 | General Line | SU | **$130** |
| Let Not Your Heart Be Troubled 610046, 2006 | General Line | OP | **$35** |
| Let the Whole World Know E7165, 1981 | General Line | SU | **$160** |

| Title | Series | Limit | Trend |
|-------|--------|-------|-------|
| Let the Whole World Know E7165, 1984+ | General Line | SU | **$100** |
| Let the Whole World Know E7165 (Fish Mark), 1983 | General Line | SU | **$120** |
| Let the Whole World Know E7165 (Hourglass Mark), 1982 | General Line | SU | **$130** |
| Let the Whole World Know E7186, 1981 | Musical | SU | **$145** |
| Let the Whole World Know E7186, 1984+ | Musical | SU | **$105** |
| Let the Whole World Know E7186 (Fish Mark), 1983 | Musical | SU | **$115** |
| Let the Whole World Know E7186 (Hourglass Mark), 1982 | Musical | SU | **$125** |
| Let Us Call the Club to Order E0103 (Fish Mark), 1983 | Collectors' Club | CL | **$50** |
| Let Us Call the Club to Order E0103 (Hourglass Mark), 1982 | Collectors' Club | CL | **$55** |
| Let Us Call the Club to Order E0303 (Cross Mark), 1984 | Collectors' Club | CL | **$45** |
| Let Us Call the Club to Order E0303 (Fish Mark), 1983 | Collectors' Club | CL | **$45** |

| Title | Series | Limit | Trend |
|-------|--------|-------|-------|
| Let Us Call the Club to Order E0303 (Hourglass Mark), 1982 | Collectors' Club | CL | **$50** |
| Let Your Gentle Spirit Be Known to All 550039, 2006 | General Line | OP | **$40** |
| Let's Always Preserve Our Friendship 114020, 2003 | General Line | OP | **$34** |
| Let's Be Friends 527270, 1990 | Birthday Series | RT | **$17** |
| Let's Have a Ball Together 889849, 2001 | Boys & Girls Clubs of America | CL | **$35** |
| Let's Keep In Touch 102520, 1986 | Musical | RT | **$84** |
| Let's Put the Pieces Together 525928, 1997 | General Line | OP | **$53** |
| Let's Sea Where This Friendship Takes Us 115654, 2004 | Sea of Friendship | RT | **$45** |
| Lettuce Pray 261122, 1997 | General Line | RT | **$18** |
| Life Can Be a Jungle 325457, 1998 | General Line | SU | **$44** |
| Life Is a Fiesta (Spain) 456381, 1998 | Little Moments International | OP | **$35** |

| Title | Series | Limit | Trend |
|---|---|---|---|
| Life Is So Uplifting 878995, 2001 | Special Wishes | OP | **$32** |
| Life Is Sweeter With You 710033, 2007 | General Line | OP | **$60** |
| Life Is Worth Fighting For 680982, 2000 | General Line | RT | **$30** |
| Life Never Smelled So Good 101547, 2002 | Smiles Forever | 5,000 | **$30** |
| Life Would Be the Pits Without Friends 795356, 2001 | Country Lane | RT | **$36** |
| Life's a Picnic With My Honey 630040, 2007 | General Line | 3,000 | **$120** |
| Life's Beary Precious With You 642673, 2001 | Special Wishes | OP | **$25** |
| Life's Filled With Little Surprises 524034, 1999 | Little Moments | CL | **$23** |
| Life's Journey Has Its Ups and Downs 521345, 2003 | Special Wishes | RT | **$35** |
| Life's Ups & Downs Are Smoother With You 104275, 2003 | General Line | OP | **$30** |

| Title | Series | Limit | Trend |
|-------|--------|-------|-------|
| Light of the World Is Jesus, The 455954, 1998 | Nativity | OP | **$30** |
| Light of the World Is Jesus, The 521507, 1988 | General Line | RT | **$64** |
| Lighted Christmas Tree 184039, 1996 | Sugar Town | RT | **$67** |
| Lighted Warming Hut 192341, 1996 | Sugar Town | RT | **$70** |
| Like Father, Like Son 115906, 2004 | General Line | OP | **$50** |
| Lily Virtuous, April 101519, 2002 | Calendar Girl | OP | **$36** |
| Little Bo Peep 729507, 2003 | Nursery Rhyme | * | **$20** |
| Little Help Goes a Long Way, A, 117796, 2004 | General Line | OP | **$40** |
| Little Miss Muffet 729493, 2003 | Nursery Rhyme | * | **$20** |
| Living Each Day With Love 103175, 2002 | Rose Petals Series/ GoCollect Exclusive | CL | **$50** |
| Llamas 531375, 1993 | Noah's Ark/ Two By Two | RT | **$19** |
| Loads of Love For Mommy 101514, 2002 | General Line | RT | **$80** |

Life Would Be the Pits Without Friends 795356, Country Lane series, 2001, **$36.**

Living Each Day With Love 103175, Rose Petals series, 2002, **$50.**

Loads of Love for My Mommy 101514, 2002, **$80.**

The Lord Bless You and Keep You E3114, 1980, **$50-$75.**

| Title | Series | Limit | Trend |
|-------|--------|-------|-------|
| Lord Bless You and Keep You waterball, The 551003, 2006 | General Line | OP | **$25** |
| Lord Bless You and Keep You, The (Bride), 2001 | General Line | * | **$28** |
| Lord Bless You and Keep You, The (Groom), 2001 | General Line | * | **$28** |
| Lord Bless You and Keep You, The 100633, 1985 | General Line | SU | **$15** |
| Lord Bless You and Keep You, The 532118, 1993 | General Line | SU | **$45** |
| Lord Bless You and Keep You, The 532126, 1993 | General Line | OP | **$24** |
| Lord Bless You and Keep You, The 532134, 1993 | General Line | SU | **$23** |
| Lord Bless You and Keep You, The E3114, 1980 | General Line | OP | **$75** |
| Lord Bless You and Keep You, The E3114, 1983+ | General Line | OP | **$50** |
| Lord Bless You and Keep You, The E3114 (Hourglass Mark), 1982 | General Line | OP | **$55** |
| Lord Bless You and Keep You, The E3114 (Triangle Mark), 1981 | General Line | OP | **$60** |

The Lord Bless You and Keep You E4721, 1980, **$35-$60.**

Lord Give Me a Song 12386, Rejoice in the Lord series, 1985, **$27.**

The Lord Giveth and the Lord Taketh Away 100226, 1987, **$44.**

Lord Keep Me On the Ball 12270, Clown series, 1986, **$30.**

| Title | Series | Limit | Trend |
|---|---|---|---|
| Lord Bless You and Keep You, The E4720, 1980 | General Line | SU | **$31** |
| Lord Bless You and Keep You, The E4721, 1980 | General Line | OP | **$60** |
| Lord Bless You and Keep You, The E4721, 1983+ | General Line | OP | **$35** |
| Lord Bless You and Keep You, The E4721 (Hourglass Mark), 1982 | General Line | OP | **$40** |
| Lord Bless You and Keep You, The E4721 (Triangle Mark), 1981 | General Line | OP | **$40** |
| Lord Bless You and Keep You, The E4721D, 2001 | General Line | OP | **$35** |
| Lord Bless You and Keep You, The E7180, 1979 | Musical | RT | **$85** |
| Lord Bless You and Keep You, The, Trinket Box E7167, 1981 | General Line | SU | **$50** |
| Lord Bless You and Keep You, The, Trinket Box E7167 (Cross Mark), 1984 | General Line | SU | **$50** |
| Lord Bless You and Keep You, The, Trinket Box E7167 (Fish Mark), 1983 | General Line | SU | **$60** |

| Title | Series | Limit | Trend |
|---|---|---|---|
| Lord Bless You and Keep You, The, Trinket Box E7167 (Hourglass Mark), 1982 | General Line | SU | **$60** |
| Lord Can Dew Anything, The 795208, 2001 | General Line | RT | **$32** |
| Lord Give Me a Song 12386, 1985 | Rejoice In the Lord | SU | **$27** |
| Lord Give Me Patience E7159 (Cross Mark), 1984 | General Line | SU | **$45** |
| Lord Give Me Patience E7159 (Fish Mark), 1983 | General Line | SU | **$45** |
| Lord Give Me Patience E7159 (Hourglass Mark), 1982 | General Line | SU | **$50** |
| Lord Giveth and the Lord Taketh Away, The 100226, 1987 | General Line | RT | **$44** |
| Lord Help Me Clean Up My Act 101545, 2002 | Smiles Forever | 5,000 | **$30** |
| Lord Help Me Make the Grade 106216, 1987 | General Line | SU | **$42** |
| Lord Help Me Stick to My Job 521450, 1989 | General Line | RT | **$37** |
| Lord Help Me to Stay On Course 532096, 1995 | General Line | RT | **$35** |
| Lord Help Us Keep Our Act Together 101850, 1987+ | General Line | RT | **$100-$125** |

| Title | Series | Limit | Trend |
|---|---|---|---|
| Lord Help Us Keep Our Act Together 101850 (Olive Branch Mark), 1986 | General Line | RT | **$115** |
| Lord I'm Coming Home 100110, 1986 | General Line | RT | **$68** |
| Lord I'm In It Again 525944, 2000 | General Line | OP | **$50** |
| Lord Is Always Bee-side Us, The 928550, 2001 | General Line | SU | **$30** |
| Lord Is Counting On You, The 531707, 1994 | General Line | RT | **$26** |
| Lord Is My Shepherd, The 523402, 1997 | Chapel Exclusive | 7,500 | **$52** |
| Lord Is My Shepherd, The PM851, 1985 | Collectors' Club | CL | **$65** |
| Lord Is Our Chief Inspiration, The 204870, 1996 | Chapel Exclusive | CL | **$220** |
| Lord Is the Hope of Our Future, The 261564, 1997 | General Line | OP | **$36** |
| Lord Is the Hope of Our Future, The 261564l, 1999 | General Line | OP | **$36** |
| Lord Is the Hope of Our Future, The 877123, 2001 | General Line | OP | **$40** |
| Lord Is the Hope of Our Future, The 877131, 2001 | General Line | OP | **$40** |

| Title | Series | Limit | Trend |
|---|---|---|---|
| Lord Is With You, The 526835, 1996 | General Line | RT | **$27** |
| Lord Is Your Light to Happiness, The 520837, 1988 | General Line | OP | **$57** |
| Lord Keep Me In Teepee Top Shape PM912, 1991 | Collectors' Club | CL | **$35** |
| Lord Keep Me On My Toes 100129, 1985 | General Line | RT | **$34** |
| Lord Keep Me On the Ball 12270, 1986 | Clown | SU | **$30** |
| Lord Keep My Life In Balance 520691, 1991 | Musical | SU | **$80** |
| Lord Keep My Life In Tune 12165, 1985 | Rejoice In the Lord | SU | **$100** |
| Lord Keep My Life In Tune 12580, 1987 | Rejoice In the Lord | SU | **$126** |
| Lord Let Our Friendship Bloom 879126, 2001 | General Line | SU | **$34** |
| Lord Please Don't Put Me On Hold PM982, 1998 | Collectors' Club | CL | **$37** |
| Lord Police Protect Us 539953, 1999 | General Line | SU | **$57** |
| Lord Spare Me 521191, 1997 | General Line | RT | **$27** |
| Lord Speak to Me 531987, 1999 | General Line | RT | **$30** |

| Title | Series | Limit | Trend |
|---|---|---|---|
| Lord Teach Us to Pray 524158, 1993 | General Line | CL | **$25** |
| Lord Turn My Life Around 520551, 1988 | General Line | SU | **$47** |
| Lord Turned My Life Around, The 520535, 1992 | General Line | SU | **$35** |
| Lord Will Carry You Through, The 12467, 1986 | Clown | RT | **$39** |
| Lord Will Provide, The 523593, 1993 | General Line | CL | **$37** |
| Love Angel and Rose Figurine 634832, 1999 | General Line | OP | **$34** |
| Love Beareth All Things E7158, 1983+ | General Line | CL | **$50** |
| Love Beareth All Things E7158 (Hourglass Mark), 1982 | General Line | CL | **$60** |
| Love Blooms Eternal 127019, 1995 | General Line | SU | **$23** |
| Love Cannot Break a True Friendship E4722, 1980 | General Line | SU | **$130** |
| Love Cannot Break a True Friendship E4722, 1984-1985 | General Line | SU | **$85** |
| Love Cannot Break a True Friendship E4722 (Fish Mark), 1983 | General Line | SU | **$90** |

Lord Help Us Keep Our Act Together 101850, 1986, **$100-$125.**

The Lord Will Carry You Through 12467, Clown series, 1986, **$39.**

Lord I'm Coming Home 100110, 1986, **$68.**

Lord Keep My Life in Tune musical 12165, Rejoice in
the Lord series, 1985, **$100.**

Lord Keep My Life In Tune 12580, Rejoice in the Lord
series, 1987, **$126.**

Love Cannot Break a True Friendship E4722, 1980, **$85-$130.**

Love Covers All thimble
12254, 1985, **$15.**

Love Covers All
12009, 1985, **$19.**

| Title | Series | Limit | Trend |
|---|---|---|---|
| Love Cannot Break a True Friendship E4722 (Hourglass Mark), 1982 | General Line | SU | **$105** |
| Love Cannot Break a True Friendship E4722 (Triangle Mark), 1981 | General Line | SU | **$115** |
| Love Covers All 12009, 1985 | General Line | SU | **$19** |
| Love Covers All thimble 12254, 1985 | General Line | SU | **$15** |
| Love From the First Impression (Boy) 115898, 2004 | General Line | OP | **$27** |
| Love From the First Impression (Girl) 115899, 2004 | General Line | OP | **$27** |
| Love Gives Me Strength to Fly CC790003, 2007 | Collectors' Club | * | **$35** |
| Love Grows Here 272981, 1997 | Easter Seals | CL | **$500** |
| Love Grows Where You Plant It 120120, 2004 | General Line | * | **$38** |
| Love Is a Heavenly Song 110367, 2003 | Easter Seals Heaven's Grace | OP | **$125** |
| Love Is a Warm Heart On a Cold Day 4024084, 2005 | General Line | OP | **$30** |
| Love Is Color Blind 524204, 1998 | Boys & Girls Clubs of America | RT | **$52** |

Love Grows Where You Plant It 120120, 2004, **$38.**

Love is Kind E1379R, 1998, **$14.**

Love is Kind E5377, 1984, **$32.**

| Title | Series | Limit | Trend |
|---|---|---|---|
| Love Is From Above 521841, 1989 | General Line | SU | **$39** |
| Love Is Kind E1379A, 1979 | General Line | SU | **$130** |
| Love Is Kind E1379A, 1980 | General Line | SU | **$130** |
| Love Is Kind E1379A (Cross Mark), 1984 | General Line | SU | **$85** |
| Love Is Kind E1379A (Fish Mark), 1983 | General Line | SU | **$85** |
| Love Is Kind E1379A (Hour-glass Mark), 1982 | General Line | SU | **$85** |
| Love Is Kind E1379A (Triangle Mark), 1981 | General Line | SU | **$100** |
| Love Is Kind E1379R, 1998 | Events | YR | **$14** |
| Love Is Kind E5377, 1984 | General Line | RT | **$32** |
| Love Is On Its Way 101544, 2002 | Smiles Forever | 5,000 | **$30** |
| Love Is Patient E9251 (Cross Decal), 1982 | General Line | SU | **$75** |
| Love Is Patient E9251, 1984-1985 | General Line | SU | **$55** |
| Love Is Patient E9251 (Fish Mark), 1983 | General Line | SU | **$70** |
| Love Is Reflected In You 0000385, 2004 | Pretty As a Princess | 10,000 | **$34** |

| Title | Series | Limit | Trend |
|-------|--------|-------|-------|
| Love Is Sharing 272493, 1996 | Baby Classics | RT | **$60** |
| Love Is Sharing E7162 (Cross Mark), 1984 | General Line | SU | **$105** |
| Love Is Sharing E7162 (Fish Mark), 1983 | General Line | SU | **$110** |
| Love Is Sharing E7162 (Hour-glass Mark), 1982 | General Line | SU | **$130** |
| Love Is Sharing E7185, 1984-1985 | Musical | RT | **$125** |
| Love Is Sharing E7185 (Fish Mark), 1983 | Musical | RT | **$155** |
| Love Is Sharing E7185 (Hour-glass Mark), 1982 | Musical | RT | **$165** |
| Love Is the Best Gift of All 110930, 1986 | Christmas Annual | YR | **$31** |
| Love Is the Best Gift of All thimble 109843, 1987 | General Line | YR | **$23** |
| Love Is the Color of Rainbows 120106, 2004 | General Line | YR | **$45** |
| Love Is the Glue That Mends 104027, 1987 | General Line | SU | **$55** |
| Love Is the Key 482242, 1999 | Avon Exclusive | YR | **$35** |
| Love Is the True Reward 108603, 2003 | Catalog Exclusive | 3,500 | **$35** |

Love is Reflected in You 0000385, Pretty as a Princess series, 2004, **$34.**

Love is Sharing E7162, 1982, **$105-$130.**

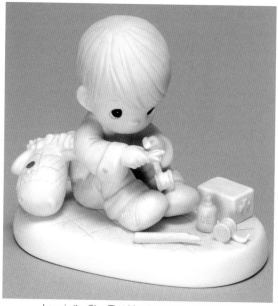

Love is the Glue That Mends 104027, 1987, **$55.**

Love Lifted Me E1375A, 1979, one of the Original 21 figurines, **$60-$140.**

| Title | Series | Limit | Trend |
|-------|--------|-------|-------|
| Love Is Universal 192376, 1997 | Easter Seals | CL | **$600** |
| Love Letters In the Sand 129488, 1997 | General Line | RT | **$40** |
| Love Lifted Me E1375A, 1979 | General Line | RT | **$140** |
| Love Lifted Me E1375A, 1980 | General Line | RT | **$140** |
| Love Lifted Me E1375A, 1984+ | General Line | RT | **$60** |
| Love Lifted Me E1375A (Fish Mark), 1983 | General Line | RT | **$70** |
| Love Lifted Me E1375A (Hourglass Mark), 1982 | General Line | RT | **$80** |
| Love Lifted Me E1375A (Triangle Mark), 1981 | General Line | RT | **$85** |
| Love Lifted Me E5201, 1980 | General Line | SU | **$100** |
| Love Lifted Me E5201 (Cross Mark), 1984 | General Line | SU | **$65** |
| Love Lifted Me E5201 (Double Triangle & Hourglass Mark), 1980 | General Line | SU | **$130** |
| Love Lifted Me E5201 (Fish Mark), 1983 | General Line | SU | **$70** |
| Love Lifted Me E5201 (Hourglass Mark), 1982 | General Line | SU | **$75** |

| Title | Series | Limit | Trend |
|---|---|---|---|
| Love Lifted Me E5201 (Triangle Mark), 1981 | General Line | SU | **$80** |
| Love Like No Other, A 681075, 1999 | Motherhood | OP | **$40** |
| Love Makes the World Go 'Round 139475, 1995 | Century Circle | CL | **$360** |
| Love Never Fails 12300, 1985 | General Line | RT | **$55** |
| Love Never Leaves a Mother's Arms 523941, 1996 | General Line | OP | **$36** |
| Love One Another 272507, 1996 | Baby Classics | RT | **$30** |
| Love One Another 822426, 2001 | Easter Seals | 1,500 | **$500** |
| Love One Another Box 488410, 1998 | General Line | OP | **$25** |
| Love One Another E1376, 1979 | General Line | OP | **$120** |
| Love One Another E1376, 1980 | General Line | OP | **$120** |
| Love One Another E1376, 1983+ | General Line | OP | **$50** |
| Love One Another E1376 (Hourglass Mark), 1982 | General Line | OP | **$55** |
| Love One Another E1376 (Triangle Mark), 1981 | General Line | OP | **$70** |

| Title | Series | Limit | Trend |
|---|---|---|---|
| Love One Another LE2001, 2001 | Easter Seals | LE | **$515** |
| Love Pacifies BC911, 1991 | Birthday Club | CL | **$29** |
| Love Rescued Me 102393, 1986 | General Line | RT | **$36** |
| Love Vows to Always Bloom 129097, 1995 | To Have & to Hold | SU | **$48** |
| Love Will Carry You Through 4001246, 2004 | General Line | OP | **$45** |
| Love's Russian Into My Heart (Russia) 456446, 1998 | Little Moments International | OP | **$27** |
| Loving Heart Is Forever, A 4004679, 2005 | General Line | OP | **$35** |
| Loving Is Caring 320579, 1997 | Little Moments | OP | **$20** |
| Loving Is Caring 320595, 1997 | Little Moments | OP | **$18** |
| Loving Is Sharing 272493, 1996 | General Line | RT | **$25** |
| Loving Is Sharing E3110B, 1980 | General Line | RT | **$120** |
| Loving Is Sharing E3110B, 1984+ | General Line | RT | **$50** |
| Loving Is Sharing E3110B (Fish Mark), 1983 | General Line | RT | **$55** |

Love Lifted Me E5201, 1980, **$65-$130.**

A Love Like No Other 681075, Motherhood series, 1999, **$40.**

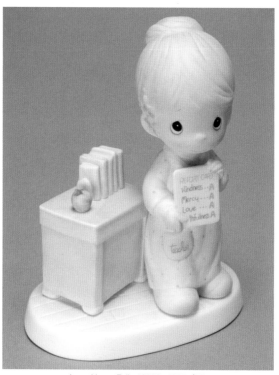

Love Never Fails 12300, 1985, **$55.**

Love Never Leaves a Mother's Arms 523941, 1996, **$36.**

Love One Another E1376, 1979, one of the Original 21 figurines,
**$50-$120.**

| Title | Series | Limit | Trend |
|---|---|---|---|
| Loving Is Sharing E3110B (Hourglass Mark), 1982 | General Line | RT | **$90** |
| Loving Is Sharing E3110B (Triangle Mark), 1981 | General Line | RT | **$95** |
| Loving Is Sharing E3110G, 1980 | General Line | RT | **$95** |
| Loving Is Sharing E3110G, 1983+ | General Line | RT | **$35-$70** |
| Loving Is Sharing E3110G (Hourglass Mark), 1982 | General Line | RT | **$80** |
| Loving Is Sharing E3110G (Triangle Mark), 1981 | General Line | RT | **$85** |
| Loving PM932, 1993 | Collectors' Club | CL | **$39** |
| Loving You Dear Valentine 306932, 1997 | Baby Classics | RT | **$17** |
| Loving You Dear Valentine PM873, 1987 | Collectors' Club | CL | **$40** |
| Loving You Dear Valentine PM874, 1987 | Collectors' Club | CL | **$45** |
| Loving, Caring and Sharing Along the Way C0013, 1993 | Collectors' Club | CL | **$27** |
| Loving, Caring and Sharing Along the Way C0113, 1993 | Collectors' Club | CL | **$27** |

| Title | Series | Limit | Trend |
|---|---|---|---|
| Loving, Caring and Shearing 898414, 2001 | Show Exclusive | CL | **$58** |
| Lovingcaringsharing.com 679860, 1999 | Special Wishes | OP | **$35** |
| Luggage Cart With Kitten 150185, 1995 | Sugar Town | RT | **$10** |
| Luke 2:10-11 532916, 1994 | General Line | RT | **$38** |
| Magic of the Season, The 710050, 2007 | Disney | OP | **$56** |
| Magically Ever After 620030, | Disney Showcase Collection | OP | **$70** |
| Maid of Honor (African-American) 902039, 2002 | General Line | OP | **$25** |
| Maid of Honor (Asian) 902055, 2002 | General Line | OP | **$25** |
| Maid of Honor (Hispanic) 901571, 2001 | General Line | SU | **$38** |
| Mailbox 531847, 1994 | Sugar Town | RT | **$8** |
| Make a Joyful Noise 272450, 1996 | Baby Classics | RT | **$23** |
| Make a Joyful Noise 520322, 1989 | Easter Seals | CL | **$866** |
| Make a Joyful Noise 528617, 1992 | General Line | CL | **$29** |

Love Rescued Me 102393, 1986, **$36.**

Loving is Sharing E3110B, 1980, **$50-$120.**

Loving is Sharing E3110G, 1980, **$35-$95.**

Make a Joyful Noise E1374G, 1979, **$100.**

| Title | Series | Limit | Trend |
|---|---|---|---|
| Make a Joyful Noise Covered Box 488402, 1998 | General Line | OP | **$44** |
| Make a Joyful Noise E1374G, 1979 | General Line | RT | **$100** |
| Make a Joyful Noise E1374G, 1980 | General Line | RT | **$100** |
| Make a Joyful Noise E1374G, 1983+ | General Line | RT | **$35-$60** |
| Make a Joyful Noise E1374G (Hourglass Mark), 1982 | General Line | RT | **$70** |
| Make a Joyful Noise E1374G (Triangle Mark), 1981 | General Line | RT | **$70** |
| Make Every Day Magical 4004159, 2006 | Disney Showcase Collection | OP | **$45** |
| Make Everything a Masterpiece 4001571, 2005 | Premier Collection | 3,000 | **$135** |
| Make Me a Blessing 100102, 1986 | General Line | RT | **$45** |
| Make Me Strong 481688, 1998 | Special Wishes | CL | **$60** |
| Make Time For Loving, Caring and Sharing (3 pieces) 118872, 118873, 118874, 2004 | Century Circle | 3,500 | **$90** |
| Making a Point to Say You're Special BC951, 1995 | Birthday Club | CL | **$28** |

| Title | Series | Limit | Trend |
|---|---|---|---|
| Making a Trail to Bethlehem 142751, 1995 | Nativity | RT | **$33** |
| Making a Trail to Bethlehem 184004, 1996 | Mini Nativity | OP | **$22** |
| Making Spirits Bright 150118, 1995 | General Line | RT | **$26** |
| Many Moons In Same Canoe, Blessum You 520772 (Bow & Arrow Mark), 1989 | General Line | RT | **$310** |
| Many Moons In Same Canoe, Blessum You 520772 (Flower Mark), 1988 | General Line | RT | **$350** |
| Many Years of Blessing You 384887, 1998 | General Line | CL | **$56** |
| March 110019, 1988 | Calendar Girl | RT | **$33** |
| March 261270, 1996 | Little Moments Birthstone Collection | OP | **$20** |
| March Girl With Waterball 844292, 2001 | General Line | OP | **$30** |
| Marching Ahead to Another 25 Years of Precious Moments 108544, 2003 | 25th Anniversary | 5,000 | **$283** |

Two variations of Make a Joyful Noise E1374G, 1979, one of the Original 21 figurines, **$60-$100.**

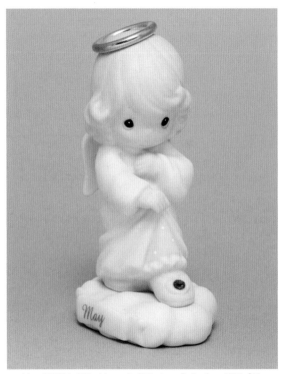

May, 261211, Little Moments Birthstone Collection, 1996, **$20.**

May Only Good Things Come Your Way 524425, 1991, **$26.**

| Title | Series | Limit | Trend |
|---|---|---|---|
| Marching to the Beat of Freedom's Drum 521981, 1996 | Special Wishes | RT | **$23** |
| Markie 528099, 1993 | Sammy's Circus | SU | **$19** |
| Marvelous Grace 325503, 1998 | General Line | CL | **$54** |
| Mary, Mary So Extraordinary 729477, 2003 | Nursery Rhyme | * | **$20** |
| May 110035, 1988 | Calendar Girl | RT | **$76** |
| May 261211, 1996 | Little Moments Birthstone Collection | OP | **$20** |
| May Girl With Waterball 844314, 2001 | General Line | OP | **$30** |
| May Love Blossom All Around You 115922, 2004 | General Line | 3,500 | **$150** |
| May Love Blossom Wherever You Go 4004738, 2005 | General Line | YR | **$50** |
| May Only Good Things Come Your Way 524425, 1991 | General Line | RT | **$26** |
| May Sweetness and Love Shower Down On You 630017, 2007 | General Line | OP | **$55** |

| Title | Series | Limit | Trend |
|-------|--------|-------|-------|
| May the Sun Always Shine On You 184217, 1996 | Century Circle | YR | **$14** |
| May You Have the Sweetest Christmas 15776, 1985 | Family Christmas | SU | **$37** |
| May Your Birthday Be a Blessing 524301, 1990 | General Line | SU | **$35** |
| May Your Birthday Be a Blessing 524301B, 2001 | General Line | SU | **$35** |
| May Your Birthday Be a Blessing E2826, 1984 | General Line | RT | **$30** |
| May Your Birthday Be Gigantic 15970, 1985 | Birthday Train | OP | **$19** |
| May Your Birthday Be Mammoth 521825, 1991 | Birthday Train | OP | **$20** |
| May Your Birthday Be Warm 15938, 1985 | Birthday Train | OP | **$15** |
| May Your Christmas Be Blessed E5376, 1984 | General Line | SU | **$37** |
| May Your Christmas Be Cozy E2345, 1982 | General Line | SU | **$65** |
| May Your Christmas Be Delightful 15482, 1985 | General Line | SU | **$34** |
| May Your Christmas Be Delightful 604135, 1997 | General Line | RT | **$55** |

| Title | Series | Limit | Trend |
|---|---|---|---|
| May Your Christmas Be Filled With Sweet Surprises 610018, 2006 | General Line | OP | **$50** |
| May Your Christmas Be Merry 524166, 1990 | Christmas Annual | SU | **$35** |
| May Your Christmas Be Merry thimble 524190, 1991 | General Line | SU | **$16** |
| May Your Christmas Be Warm E2348 (Cross Mark) 1984 | General Line | SU | **$120** |
| May Your Christmas Be Warm E2348 (Fish Mark) 1983 | General Line | SU | **$145** |
| May Your Christmas Be Warm E2348 (Hourglass Mark), 1982 | General Line | SU | **$155** |
| May Your Christmas Begin With a Bang 877433, 2001 | General Line | CL | **$28** |
| May Your Days Be Merry and Bright 117856, 2004 | General Line | OP | **$20** |
| May Your Days Be Merry and Bright 878901, 2001 | Christmas Remembered | OP | **$45** |
| May Your Days Be Rosy 781770C, 2001 | Century Circle | CL | **$30** |
| May Your Days Be Warm & Fuzzy 4004742, 2005 | Hallmark Exclusive | OP | **$50** |
| May Your Every Wish Come True 524298, 1992 | General Line | OP | **$50** |

May You Have the Sweetest Christmas 15776, Family Christmas, 1985, **$37.**

May Your Birthday Be a Blessing E2826, 1984, **$30.**

May Your Birthday Be Gigantic 15970, Birthday Train, 1985, **$19.**

May Your Christmas Be Delightful 604135, 1997, **$55.**

May Your Christmas Be Filled With Sweet Surprises 610018, 2006, **$50.**

| Title | Series | Limit | Trend |
|---|---|---|---|
| May Your Faith Grow With Daily Care 108540, 2003 | General Line | OP | **$36** |
| May Your Future Be Blessed 525316, 1992 | General Line | OP | **$35** |
| May Your Heart Be Filled With Christmas Joy 112880, 2003 | General Line | OP | **$45** |
| May Your Holidays Be Filled With Christmas Cheer 0000860 | General Line | * | **$45** |
| May Your Holidays Be So-Sew Special 4024088, 2005 | General Line | YR | **$35** |
| May Your Holidays Sparkle With Joy 104202, 2002 | General Line | YR | **$35** |
| May Your Life Be Blessed With Touchdowns 522023, 1989 | General Line | RT | **$60** |
| May Your Life Be Blessed With Touchdowns 522023 (Missing Leaf), 1989 | General Line | RT | **$110** |
| May Your Prayers Be Answered 283452, 2005 | Hallmark Exclusive | OP | **$30** |
| May Your Season Be Jelly and Bright 587885, 1999 | General Line | OP | **$34** |
| May Your World Be Filled With Love 610058, 2006 | General Line | OP | **$50** |
| May Your World Be Trimmed With Joy 522082, 1990 | General Line | SU | **$45** |

May Your Christmas Be Warm E2348, 1982, **$120-$155.**

May Your Holidays Be So-Sew Special 4024088, 2005, **$35.**

| Title | Series | Limit | Trend |
|-------|--------|-------|-------|
| Mazie 184055, 1996 | Sugar Town | RT | **$35** |
| Memories Are Made of This 529982, 1994 | Events | YR | **$26** |
| Meowie Christmas 109800, 1988 | General Line | RT | **$64** |
| Merry Christmas Deer 522317, 1989 | General Line | RT | **$82** |
| Merry Christmas Two Ewe 4003168, 2005 | General Line | OP | **$35** |
| Merry Christ-Miss 104218, 2002 | General Line | OP | **$32** |
| Merry Go Round 272841, 1997 | Sugar Town | RT | **$34** |
| Mi Pequeno Amor (My Little Sweetheart) 928461, 2001 | General Line | OP | **$40** |
| Mini Baby Boy Crawling 119920, 2004 | General Line | OP | **$18** |
| Mini Baby Boy Kneeling 119917, 2004 | General Line | OP | **$18** |
| Mini Baby Boy Standing 119916, 2004 | General Line | SU | **$18** |
| Mini Baby Girl Crawling 119921, 2004 | General Line | OP | **$18** |
| Mini Baby Girl Sitting 119919, 2004 | General Line | OP | **$18** |

May Your Season Be Jelly and Bright 587885, 1999, **$34.**

Merry Christmas Deer 522317, 1989, **$82.**

| Title | Series | Limit | Trend |
|-------|--------|-------|-------|
| Mini Baby Girl Standing 119918, 2004 | General Line | SU | **$18** |
| Miniature waterball 701041, 1999 | General Line | CL | **$10** |
| Miracles Can Happen 994871, 2002 | Animal Affections | OP | **$20** |
| Missing You 524107, 2001 | Special Wishes | OP | **$30** |
| Missum You 306991, 1998 | General Line | RT | **$42** |
| Mixing Up a Brighter Tomorrow 4004740, 2005 | Through the Years | 7,500 | **$45** |
| Mom, You Always Make Our House a Home 325465, 1998 | General Line | SU | **$39** |
| Mom, You Are a Bouquet of Love and Understanding 640003, 2007 | General Line | OP | **$55** |
| Mom, You Are a Royal Gem 588083, 1999 | Avon Exclusive | YR | **$30** |
| Mom, You're a Sweetheart 104850, 2002 | Avon Exclusive | OP | **$20** |
| Mom, You're My Special-Tea 325473, 1999 | Mother's Day | RT | **$24** |
| Mom, You're Never Too Close For Comfort 690021, 2007 | General Line | OP | **$40** |

Mom, You're a Sweetheart 2002 104850, Avon exclusive, 2002, **$20.**

| Title | Series | Limit | Trend |
|---|---|---|---|
| Mom, You've Given Me So Much 488046, 1999 | General Line | OP | **$30** |
| Mommy and Me (Boy) 115900, 2004 | General Line | OP | **$25** |
| Mommy and Me (Girl) 115901, 2004 | General Line | OP | **$25** |
| Mommy, I Love You 109975, 1987 | General Line | RT | **$31** |
| Mommy, I Love You 112143, 1987 | General Line | RT | **$40** |
| Mommy's Little Angel (Blonde Boy) 888001, 2002 | General Line | OP | **$25** |
| Mommy's Little Angel (Blonde Girl) 111870, 2003 | General Line | OP | **$23** |
| Mommy's Little Angel (Brunette Boy) 887994, 2002 | General Line | OP | **$19** |
| Mommy's Little Angel (Brunette Girl) 111869, 2003 | General Line | OP | **$23** |
| Mommy's Love Goes With You 690007, 2007 | Chapel Exclusive | 1,500 | **$50** |
| Moms Are the Greatest Gift of All 550011, 2006 | General Line | OP | **$45** |
| Monarch Is Born, A E5380, 1984 | Nativity | SU | **$70** |
| Monday's Child Is Fair of Face 692085, 2001 | Days of the Week | OP | **$18** |

| Title | Series | Limit | Trend |
|---|---|---|---|
| Money's Not the Only Green Thing Worth Saving 531073, 1994 | General Line | RT | **$36** |
| Mornin' Pumpkin 455687, 1998 | General Line | RT | **$49** |
| Morning Glory Easily Contented, September 101525, 2002 | Calendar Girl | OP | **$36** |
| Most Precious Gift of All, The 183814, 1997 | General Line | RT | **$44** |
| Most Precious Gift of All, The (Green Dress) 183814S, 1996 | General Line | YR | **$18** |
| Mother Sew Dear E3106, 1980 | General Line | RT | **$55** |
| Mother Sew Dear E3106, 1983-1985 | General Line | RT | **$35** |
| Mother Sew Dear E3106 (Hourglass Mark), 1982 | General Line | RT | **$45** |
| Mother Sew Dear E3106 (Triangle Mark), 1981 | General Line | RT | **$50** |
| Mother Sew Dear E7182, 1982 | Musical | RT | **$71** |
| Mother Sew Dear thimble 13293, 1985 | General Line | RT | **$30** |

| Title | Series | Limit | Trend |
|---|---|---|---|
| Mother's Arms Are Always Open, A, 118444, 2004 | General Line | OP | **$45** |
| Mother's Love Grows By Giving, A 640004, 2007 | General Line | OP | **$60** |
| Mother's Love Is a Warm Glow, A 4001650, 2005 | General Line | SU | **$45** |
| Mother's Love Is Beyond Measure, A 113037, 2003 | General Line | OP | **$40** |
| Mother's Love Is From Above, A 104311, 2003 | Motherhood | OP | **$40** |
| Mow Power to You PM892, 1989 | Collectors' Club | CL | **$32** |
| Mr. Fujioka 781851, 2000 | Events | RT | **$22** |
| Musical Bridal Arch 876151, 2001 | General Line | OP | **$50** |
| My Collection PM001, 2000 | Collectors' Club | CL | **$20** |
| My Cup Runneth Over 610051, 2006 | General Line | OP | **$45** |
| My Days Are Blue Without You 520802, 1989 | General Line | SU | **$109** |
| My Dream Boat 610071, 2006 | General Line | CL | **$100** |
| My Faith Is In Jesus 550007, 2006 | General Line | OP | **$30** |

| Title | Series | Limit | Trend |
|---|---|---|---|
| My Guardian Angel E5205, 1981 | Musical | SU | **$95** |
| My Guardian Angel E5206, 1981 | Musical | SU | **$105** |
| My Guardian Angel nightlight E5207, 1980 | General Line | SU | **$245** |
| My Happiness C0010, 1989 | Collectors' Club | CL | **$29** |
| My Happiness C0110, 1990 | Collectors' Club | CL | **$35** |
| My Heart Belongs to You 110268, 2003 | Show Exclusive | OP | **$113** |
| My Heart Is Exposed With Love 520624, 1988 | General Line | RT | **$55** |
| My Last One For You 120104, 2004 | General Line | LE | **$34** |
| My Life Is a Vacuum Without You 587907, 1999 | General Line | SU | **$34** |
| My Love Blooms For You 521728, 1996 | General Line | OP | **$33** |
| My Love Spills Over For You Mom (Girl) 101513, 2002 | Mother's Day | RT | **$35** |

Mom, You're My Special-Tea 325473, Mother's Day series, 1999, **$24.**

Mommy, I Love You 109975, 1987, **$31.**

Mommy, I Love You 112143, 1987, **$40.**

Mommy's Little Angel 888001, 2002, **$25.**

Moms Are the Greatest Gift of All 550011, 2006, **$45.**

Mornin' Pumpkin 455687, 1998, **$49.**

The Most Precious Gift of
All 183814S, 1996, **$18.**

Mother Sew Dear thimble
13293, 1985, **$30.**

Mother Sew
Dear E3106,
1980, **$35-$55.**

Mother Sew
Dear musical
E7182, 1982,
**$71.**

A Mother's Arms Are Always Open 118444, 2004, **$45.**

A Mother's Love is From Above 104311, Motherhood series, 2003, **$40.**

A Mother's Love is Beyond Measure 113037 and frame, 2003, **$40**

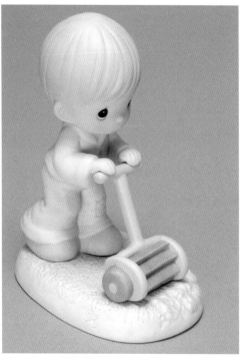

Mow Power To Ya PM892, Precious Moments Collectors'
Club, 1989, **$32.**

My Days Are Blue Without You 520802, 1989, **$109.**

My Guardian Angel boy E5205 and My Guardian Angel girl E5206, 1981, **$90** and **$105,** respectively.

| Title | Series | Limit | Trend |
|---|---|---|---|
| My Love Will Keep You Warm (No Cat) 272957S, 1998 | General Line | YR | **$29** |
| My Love Will Keep You Warm 272957, 1998 | Catalog Exclusive | OP | **$34** |
| My Love Will Never Let You Go 103497, 1986 | General Line | RT | **$26** |
| My Love Will Stand Guard Over You (England) 456934, 1998 | Little Moments International | OP | **$28** |
| My Mona Lisa 550012, 2006 | General Line | 10,000 | **$45** |
| My Most Precious Mom-ents Are With You 108528, 2003 | General Line | OP | **$36** |
| My Most Precious Mom-ents Are With You E1507, 2003 | General Line | * | **$40** |
| My Peace I Give Unto Thee 610047, 2006 | General Line | OP | **$35** |
| My True Love Gave to Me 529273, 1996 | General Line | RT | **$14** |
| My True Love Gave to Me 610011, 2006 | General Line | OP | **$50** |
| My Universe Is You 487902, 1999 | General Line | RT | **$47** |
| My Warmest Thoughts Are You 524085, 1992 | General Line | RT | **$92** |

| Title | Series | Limit | Trend |
|-------|--------|-------|-------|
| My World's Upside Down Without You 531014, 1998 | Birthday Series | OP | **$18** |
| Nativity 4003328, 2005 | Nativity | OP | **$32** |
| Nativity 529508, 1992 | Sugar Town | RT | **$45** |
| Nativity Buildings & Tree E2387, 1982 | Mini Nativity | SU | **$120** |
| Nativity Cart 528072, 1994 | Nativity | RT | **$20** |
| Nativity Wall 283436, 1997 | Mini Nativity | SU | **$40** |
| Nativity Wall E5644 (set of 2), 1981 | Nativity | OP | **$143** |
| Nearer to the Heart of God 890731, 2002 | General Line | RT | **$40** |
| Nighty Night 630022, 2007 | Picture Perfect Moments | OP | **$20** |
| No Bones About It, You're Grrreat 795321, 2001 | Special Wishes | SU | **$40** |
| No Rest For the Weary 114012, 2003 | General Line | OP | **$32** |
| No Tears Past the Gate 101826, 1986 | General Line | SU | **$90** |

My Life is a Vacuum Without You 587907, 1999, **$34.**

My Love Will Keep You Warm 272957, 1998, **$34.**

My Love Will Keep You Warm 272957S, 1998, **$29.**

My Most Precious Mom-ents Are With You 108528, 2003, **$36.**

My True Love Gave to Me 529273, 1996, **$14.**

My Universe is You 487902, 1999, **$47.**

My Warmest Thoughts Are You 524085, 1992, **$92.**

No Bones About It, You're Grrreat 795321, Special Wishes series, 2001, **$40.**

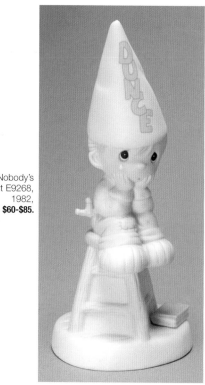

Nobody's Perfect E9268, 1982, **$60-$85.**

O, How I Love Jesus E1380B, 1979, one of the Original 21
figurines, **$85-$140.**

| Title | Series | Limit | Trend |
|---|---|---|---|
| Noah, His Wife & Ark 530042, 1993 | Noah's Ark/ Two By Two | RT | **$263** |
| Noah's Ark 8-pc. Collectors Set 530948, 1993 | Noah's Ark/ Two By Two | RT | **$218** |
| Nobody Likes to Be Dumped 307041, 1998 | Country Lane | RT | **$120** |
| Nobody's Perfect E9268, 1984+ | General Line | RT | **$60** |
| Nobody's Perfect E9268 (Fish Mark), 1983 | General Line | RT | **$80** |
| Nobody's Perfect E9268 (Hourglass Mark), 1982 | General Line | RT | **$85** |
| Nobody's Perfect E9268 (Hourglass Mark, Smiling Dunce), 1982 | General Line | RT | **$355** |
| Not a Creature Was Stirring 524484, 1989 | Birthday Series | SU | **$17** |
| Note to Self: Take Time For Me 118266, 2004 | General Line | RT | **$34** |
| Nothing Can Dampen the Spirit of Caring 603864, 1994 | Good Samaritan | RT | **$24** |
| Nothing Is Stronger Than Our Love 114023, 2004 | General Line | OP | **$27** |
| Nothing Is Tweeter Than You 954136, 2002 | Little Moments | * | **$20** |

| Title | Series | Limit | Trend |
|---|---|---|---|
| November 110108, 1988 | Calendar Girl | RT | **$32** |
| November 261297, 1996 | Little Moments Birthstone Collection | OP | **$20** |
| November Girl With waterball 844381, 2001 | General Line | OP | **$30** |
| Now I Lay Me Down to Sleep 522058, 1994 | General Line | RT | **$20** |
| Nurses Are Blessed With Patients 101554, 2002 | Little Moments | OP | **$20** |
| Nurse's Care Is the Best Medicine, A 112845, 2003 | Special Wishes | OP | **$30** |
| O Come All Ye Faithful E2352, 1982 | Musical | SU | **$122** |
| O Come All Ye Faithful E2353, 1984-1986 | General Line | RT | **$50** |
| O Come All Ye Faithful E2353 (Fish Mark), 1983 | General Line | RT | **$55** |
| O Come All Ye Faithful E2353 (Hourglass Mark), 1982 | General Line | RT | **$90** |
| O Come Let Us Adore Him 111333, 1987 | Nativity | SU | **$195** |

| Title | Series | Limit | Trend |
|-------|--------|-------|-------|
| O Holy Night 879428, 2001 | General Line | CL | **$375** |
| O Holy Night E2381R, 2003 | Mini Nativity | OP | **$14** |
| O How I Love Jesus E1380B, 1979-1980 | General Line | RT | **$140** |
| O How I Love Jesus E1380B (Cross Mark), 1984 | General Line | RT | **$85** |
| O How I Love Jesus E1380B (Fish Mark), 1983 | General Line | RT | **$90** |
| O How I Love Jesus E1380B (Hourglass Mark), 1982 | General Line | RT | **$95** |
| O How I Love Jesus E1380B (Triangle Mark), 1981 | General Line | RT | **$110** |
| O Worship the Lord 100064, 1985 | General Line | OP | **$65** |
| O Worship the Lord 102229, 1986 | General Line | RT | **$26** |
| October 110094, 1988 | Calendar Girl | RT | **$58** |
| October 261262, 1996 | Little Moments Birthstone Collection | OP | **$20** |
| October Girl With Waterball 844373, 2001 | General Line | OP | **$30** |

| Title | Series | Limit | Trend |
|-------|--------|-------|-------|
| O-fish-ally Friends For a Lifetime 795305, 2001 | General Line | OP | **$45** |
| Oh Holy Night 522546, 1988 | Christmas Annual | RT | **$40** |
| Oh Holy Night thimble 522554, 1989 | General Line | RT | **$25** |
| Oh Taste and See That the Lord Is Good 307025, 1998 | Country Lane | RT | **$41** |
| Oh What Fun It Is to Ride 109819, 1987 | General Line | RT | **$111** |
| Oh Worship the Lord E5385, 1984 | Mini Nativity | SU | **$58** |
| Oh Worship the Lord E5386, 1984 | Mini Nativity | SU | **$75** |
| Oh, What a Wonder-Fall Day 879096, 2001 | Country Lane | SU | **$40** |
| Oinky Birthday 524506, 1994 | Birthday Series | RT | **$12** |
| Old Woman In a Shoe 729469, 2003 | Nursery Rhyme | OP | **$20** |
| On a Scale From 1 to 10, You Are the Deerest 878944, 2001 | General Line | RT | **$40** |
| On a Wing and a Prayer 120115, 2004 | General Line | OP | **$36** |

| Title | Series | Limit | Trend |
|---|---|---|---|
| On My Way to a Perfect Day 522872, 1997 | General Line | RT | **$43** |
| On Our Way to a Special Day (Boy) 481602, 1998 | Special Wishes | CL | **$17** |
| On Our Way to a Special Day (Girl) 481610, 1998 | Special Wishes | CL | **$22** |
| Once Upon a Holy Night 523836, 1989 | Christmas Annual | CL | **$38** |
| Once Upon a Holy Night thimble 523844, 1990 | General Line | CL | **$20** |
| One Small Step 4004741, 2005 | Through the Years | 7,500 | **$45** |
| One Step At a Time PM911, 1991 | Collectors' Club | CL | **$42** |
| Only Love Can Make a Home PM921, 1992 | Collectors' Club | CL | **$48** |
| Only One Life to Offer 325309, 1998 | General Line | RT | **$39** |
| Only You 550000, 2006 | General Line | OP | **$50** |
| Onward Christian Soldiers E0523 (Fish Mark Stamped), 1983 | General Line | RT | **$95** |
| Onward Christian Soldiers E0523 (Fish Mark), 1983 | General Line | RT | **$55** |

October 110094, Calendar Girl series, 1988, **$58.**

On a Scale From
1 to 10 You
Are the Deerest
878944, 2001,
**$40.**

Onward Christian Soldiers E0523, 1983, **$55-$95.**

| Title | Series | Limit | Trend |
|---|---|---|---|
| Opal—Color of Happiness October 335657, 1997 | Birthstone | OP | **$25** |
| Open Your Eyes to All His Blessings 120116, 2004 | General Line | OP | **$36** |
| Orange You the Sweetest Thing 115913, 2004 | Fruitful Delights | 7,500 | **$34** |
| Our Club Can't Be Beat B0001, 1986 | Birthday Club | CL | **$43** |
| Our Club Is a Tough Act to Follow B0005, 1990 | Birthday Club | CL | **$29** |
| Our Club Is a Tough Act to Follow B0105, 1990 | Birthday Club | CL | **$30** |
| Our Club Is Soda-Licious PM962, 1996 | Collectors' Club | CL | **$36** |
| Our First Christmas Together 101702, 1986 | Musical | RT | **$77** |
| Our First Christmas Together 115290, 1988 | General Line | SU | **$42** |
| Our First Christmas Together E2377, 1982 | General Line | SU | **$69** |
| Our Friendship Goes a Long Way 531626, 2002 | Friendship | RT | **$78** |
| Our Friendship Has Always Been Write On 120119, 2004 | General Line | RT | **$23** |

| Title | Series | Limit | Trend |
|---|---|---|---|
| Our Friendship Is Always In Bloom (Japan) 456926, 1998 | Little Moments International | OP | **$45** |
| Our Friendship Is Like a Breath of Fresh Air 4004683, 2005 | General Line | OP | **$28** |
| Our Friendship Is Soda-licious 524336, 1993 | General Line | RT | **$77** |
| Our Friendship Was Made to Order 879134, 2001 | General Line | SU | **$32** |
| Our Friendship's In the Bag 119094, 2004 | General Line | OP | **$27** |
| Our Future Is Looking Much Brighter 325511, 1998 | General Line | YR | **$398** |
| Our Heroes In the Sky 958832, 2002 | Special Wishes | SU | **$32** |
| Our Heroes In the Sky 958840, 2002 | Special Wishes | OP | **$35** |
| Our Love Can Never Be Broken 550010, 2006 | General Line | OP | **$50** |
| Our Love Is Built On a Strong Foundation 114017, 2003 | General Line | OP | **$32** |
| Our Love Is Heaven Sent 101546, 2002 | Smiles Forever | 5,000 | **$30** |
| Our Love Still Sparkles In Your Eyes 115911, 2004 | General Line | OP | **$45** |

Our Club Can't Be Beat B0001, Precious Moments Birthday Club, 1986, **$43.**

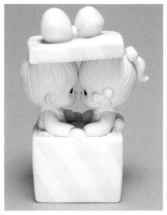

Our First Christmas Together musical 101702, 1986, **$77.**

Our First Christmas Together E2377, 1982, **$69.**

Our Friendship's in the Bag 119094, 2004, **$27.**

Our Friendship is Soda-Licious 524336, 1993, **$77.**

Our Love Can Never Be Broken 550010, 2006, **$50.**

Our Love is Built on a Strong Foundation 114017, 2003, **$32.**

Overflowing With Love 108523, 2003, **$25.**

Part of Me Wants
to Be Good 12149,
1985, **$84.**

| Title | Series | Limit | Trend |
|---|---|---|---|
| Our Love Was Meant to Be 115909, 2004 | General Line | OP | **$45** |
| Our Love Will Flow Eternal 588059, 1999 | Chapel Exclusive | OP | **$81** |
| Our Love Will Never Be Endangered 824119, 2001 | Century Circle | CL | **$100** |
| Overalls, I Think You're Special 898147, 2002 | Country Lane | RT | **$40** |
| Overflowing With Love 108523, 2003 | General Line | OP | **$25** |
| Owl Always Be There For You 104271, 2002 | General Line | SU | **$23** |
| Owl Always Be Your Friend BC932, 1993 | Birthday Club | CL | **$27** |
| Palm Trees, Hay Bail, Baby Food 272582, 1997 | Nativity | OP | **$60** |
| Part of Me Wants to Be Good 12149, 1985 | General Line | SU | **$84** |
| Part of Your World 630039, 2007 | Disney Showcase Collection | OP | **$60** |
| Peace Amid the Storm E4723, 1980 | General Line | SU | **$95** |
| Peace Amid the Storm E4723 (Cross Mark), 1984 | General Line | SU | **$70** |

| Title | Series | Limit | Trend |
|---|---|---|---|
| Peace Amid the Storm E4723 (Fish Mark), 1983 | General Line | SU | **$70** |
| Peace Amid the Storm E4723 (Hourglass Mark), 1982 | General Line | SU | **$75** |
| Peace Amid the Storm E4723 (Triangle Mark), 1981 | General Line | SU | **$85** |
| Peace In the Valley 649929, 1999 | Show Exclusive | CL | **$120** |
| Peace On Earth 109746, 1988 | Musical | SU | **$119** |
| Peace On Earth 117857, 2004 | General Line | * | **$20** |
| Peace On Earth E2804, 1980 | General Line | SU | **$155** |
| Peace On Earth E2804 (Cross Mark), 1984 | General Line | SU | **$125** |
| Peace On Earth E2804 (Fish Mark), 1983 | General Line | SU | **$130** |
| Peace On Earth E2804 (Hourglass Mark), 1982 | General Line | SU | **$135** |
| Peace On Earth E2804 (Triangle Mark), 1981 | General Line | SU | **$145** |
| Peace On Earth E2804R, 1999 | Catalog Exclusive | RT | **$63** |
| Peace On Earth E4725, 1980 | General Line | SU | **$105** |
| Peace On Earth E4725 (Cross Mark), 1984 | General Line | SU | **$55** |

| Title | Series | Limit | Trend |
|---|---|---|---|
| Peace On Earth E4725 (Fish Mark), 1983 | General Line | SU | **$60** |
| Peace On Earth E4725 (Hourglass Mark), 1982 | General Line | SU | **$70** |
| Peace On Earth E4725 (Triangle Mark), 1981 | General Line | SU | **$80** |
| Peace On Earth E4726, 1980 | Musical | SU | **$100** |
| Peace On Earth E4726 (Cross Mark), 1984 | Musical | SU | **$105** |
| Peace On Earth E4726 (Fish Mark), 1983 | Musical | SU | **$110** |
| Peace On Earth E4726 (Hourglass Mark), 1982 | Musical | SU | **$115** |
| Peace On Earth E4726 (Triangle Mark), 1981 | Musical | SU | **$120** |
| Peace On Earth E9287, 1982 | General Line | SU | **$106** |
| Peace On Earth...Anyway 183342, 1996 | Christmas Annual | YR | **$28** |
| Peace That Passes Understanding, The (7 pcs.) 730173, 2001 | Century Circle | CL | **$125** |
| Peace, Love & Joy Angels, set of 3, PML1664, 1665, 1666, 2004 | General Line | 10,000 | **$135** |
| Peace, Love & Joy 112418, 2003 | General Line | * | **$28** |

| Title | Series | Limit | Trend |
|---|---|---|---|
| Pearl of Great Price, The 526061, 1997 | Century Circle | YR | **$64** |
| Pearl—Color of Love June 335592, 1997 | Birthstone | OP | **$25** |
| Peas On Earth 455768, 1998 | General Line | RT | **$33** |
| Peas Pass the Carrots 307076, 1998 | Country Lane | RT | **$29** |
| Penny a Kiss, A Penny a Hug, A 101234, 2002 | Events | CL | **$35** |
| Perfect Display of 15 Happy Years, A 127817, 1995 | Collectors' Club | CL | **$137** |
| Perfect Grandpa, The E7160, 1984-1986 | General Line | SU | **$65** |
| Perfect Grandpa, The E7160 (Fish Mark), 1983 | General Line | SU | **$70** |
| Perfect Grandpa, The E7160 (Hourglass Mark), 1982 | General Line | SU | **$80** |
| Perfect Harmony 521914, 1994 | General Line | RT | **$37** |
| Peridot—Color of Pride August 335614, 1997 | Birthstone | OP | **$25** |
| Philip 529494, 1992 | Sugar Town | RT | **$25** |

Peace Amid the Storm E4723, 1980, **$70-$95.**

Peace on Earth E9287, 1982, **$106.**

Peas on Earth 455768, 1998, **$33.**

The Perfect Grandpa E7160, 1982, **$65-$80.**

| Title | Series | Limit | Trend |
|---|---|---|---|
| Picture's Worth a Thousand Words, A 550045, 2006 | General Line | OP | **$40** |
| Pig E9267F, | Animal Collection | SU | **$15** |
| Piggy Bank 104832, 2002 | Collectors' Club | * | **$15** |
| Pigs 530085, 1993 | Noah's Ark/ Two By Two | RT | **$15** |
| Pizza On Earth 521884, 1997 | General Line | RT | **$37** |
| Planting the Seeds of Love 101548, 2002 | Century Circle | 7,500 | **$100** |
| Poppy For You, A 604208, 1995 | General Line | SU | **$35** |
| Poppy Peaceful, August 101523, 2002 | Calendar Girl | OP | **$35** |
| Portrait of Loving, Caring and Sharing, A 108543, 2003 | Collectors' Club | LE | **$375** |
| Potty Time 531022, 1997 | General Line | RT | **$30** |
| Praise God From Whom All Blessings Flow 455695, 1998 | General Line | RT | **$37** |
| Praise Him With Resounding Cymbals 4001572, 2005 | Premier Collection | 3,000 | **$115** |
| Praise the Lord and Dosie-Do 455733, 1998 | General Line | OP | **$50** |

| Title | Series | Limit | Trend |
|---|---|---|---|
| Praise the Lord Anyhow E1374B, 1979 | General Line | RT | **$110** |
| Praise the Lord Anyhow E1374B, 1980 | General Line | RT | **$110** |
| Praise the Lord Anyhow E1374B (Hourglass Mark, Black Nose On Dog), 1982 | General Line | RT | **$65** |
| Praise the Lord Anyhow E1374B (Hourglass Mark, Brown Nose On Dog), 1982 | General Line | RT | **$75** |
| Praise the Lord Anyhow E1374B (Triangle Mark), 1981 | General Line | RT | **$85** |
| Praise the Lord Anyhow E9254, 1985+ | General Line | RT | **$50** |
| Praise the Lord Anyhow E9254 (Cross Decal), 1984 | General Line | RT | **$150** |
| Praise the Lord Anyhow E9254 (Cross Mark), 1984 | General Line | RT | **$55** |
| Praise the Lord Anyhow E9254 (Fish Decal), 1983 | General Line | RT | **$155** |
| Praise the Lord Anyhow E9254 (Fish Mark), 1983 | General Line | RT | **$95** |
| Praise the Lord Anyhow E9254 (Hourglass Mark), 1982 | General Line | RT | **$120** |

| Title | Series | Limit | Trend |
|-------|--------|-------|-------|
| Prayer Changes Things E1375B, 1979 | General Line | SU | **$195** |
| Prayer Changes Things E1375B, 1980 | General Line | SU | **$215** |
| Prayer Changes Things E1375B (Cross Mark), 1984 | General Line | SU | **$160** |
| Prayer Changes Things E1375B (Fish Mark), 1983 | General Line | SU | **$150** |
| Prayer Changes Things E1375B (Hourglass Mark), 1982 | General Line | SU | **$160** |
| Prayer Changes Things E1375B (Triangle Mark), 1981 | General Line | SU | **$165** |
| Prayer Changes Things E5214, Bible error | General Line | SU | **$165** |
| Prayer Changes Things E5214 (Cross Mark), 1984 | General Line | SU | **$85** |
| Prayer Changes Things E5214 (Fish Mark), 1983 | General Line | SU | **$95** |
| Prayer Changes Things E5214 (Hourglass Mark), 1982 | General Line | SU | **$135** |
| Prayer Changes Things E5214 (Triangle Mark), 1981 | General Line | SU | **$155** |

| Title | Series | Limit | Trend |
|---|---|---|---|
| Precious Blossoms (January-December), 2007 | Precious Blossoms | OP | **$5 EA.** |
| Precious Friends 928542, 2002 | Special Wishes | SU | **$36** |
| Precious Grandma 101504, 2002 | General Line | OP | **$23** |
| Precious Grandpa 101505, 2002 | General Line | OP | **$23** |
| Precious Memories 106763, 1987 | General Line | OP | **$48** |
| Precious Memories E2828, 1983 | General Line | RT | **$63** |
| Precious Moments Century Circle Exclusive Gift Set GC43, 2000 | Century Circle | CL | **$475** |
| Precious Moments From the Beginning 110238, 2003 | Century Circle | LE | **$167** |
| Precious Moments In Paradise 101549, 2002 | Century Circle | LE | **$45** |
| Precious Moments Last Forever E6901, 1994 | General Line | SU | **$50** |
| Precious Moments to Remember 163848, 1995 | To Have & to Hold | OP | **$65** |
| Precious Moments Will Last Forever 681008, 2000 | General Line | RT | **$35** |

Praise the Lord Anyhow E1374B, 1979, one of the Original 21 figurines, **$65-$110.**

Praise the Lord Anyhow E9254, 1982, **$50-$150.**

Prayer Changes Things E5214, 1981, **$85-$165.**

Press On E9265, 1982, **$65-$95.**

The Purr-Fect Grandma musical
E7184, 1982, **$80.**

The Purr-Fect Grandma
thimble 13307, 1985, **$7.**

| Title | Series | Limit | Trend |
|---|---|---|---|
| Preparado Con Amor 928445, 2001 | General Line | OP | **$32** |
| Prepare Ye the Way of the Lord E0508, 1983 | Nativity | SU | **$165** |
| Press On E9265, 1984 | General Line | RT | **$65** |
| Press On E9265 (Fish Mark), 1983 | General Line | RT | **$85** |
| Press On E9265 (Hourglass Mark), 1982 | General Line | RT | **$95** |
| Pretty As a Princess 526053, 1995 | Special Wishes | OP | **$35** |
| Prince of a Guy, A 526037, 1996 | General Line | RT | **$24** |
| Puppy Love 520764, 1988 | General Line | RT | **$17** |
| Puppy Love Is From Above 106798, 1987 | General Line | RT | **$53** |
| Purr-fect Christmas Morning, The 690006, 2007 | General Line | OP | **$35** |
| Purr-fect Friends 488364, 1999 | Parade of Gifts | YR | **$26** |
| Purr-fect Grandma, The E3109 (Triangle Mark), 1981 | General Line | OP | **$75** |
| Purr-fect Grandma, The E3109, 1980 | General Line | OP | **$75** |

| Title | Series | Limit | Trend |
|---|---|---|---|
| Purr-fect Grandma, The E3109, 1983+ | General Line | OP | **$35** |
| Purr-fect Grandma, The E3109 (Hourglass Mark), 1982 | General Line | OP | **$45** |
| Purr-fect Grandma, The E7184, 1982 | Musical | SU | **$80** |
| Purr-fect Grandma, The E7242, 1984+ | General Line | SU | **$35** |
| Purr-fect Grandma, The E7242 (Fish Mark), 1983 | General Line | SU | **$40** |
| Purr-fect Grandma, The E7242 (Hourglass Mark), 1982 | General Line | SU | **$45** |
| Purr-fect Grandma, The, thimble 13307, 1985 | General Line | RT | **$7** |
| Purse-Suit of Happiness 120105, 2004 | Special Wishes | OP | **$34** |
| Put a Little Punch Into Your Birthday BC931, 1993 | Birthday Club | CL | **$27** |
| Put On a Happy Face PM822 (Cross Mark), 1984 | Collectors' Club | CL | **$145** |
| Put On a Happy Face PM822 (Fish Mark), 1983 | Collectors' Club | CL | **$160** |
| Put On a Happy Face PM822 (Hourglass Mark), 1982 | Collectors' Club | CL | **$180** |

| Title | Series | Limit | Trend |
|---|---|---|---|
| Railroad Crossing Sign 150177, 1995 | Sugar Town | RT | **$8** |
| Raisin' Cane On the Holidays 730130, 2000 | General Line | SU | **$30** |
| Rats, I Missed Your Birthday 101496, 2002 | Animal Affections | OP | **$18** |
| Reflect and Give Thanks For All Life's Bounty 4001786, 2005 | Century Circle Carousel | 2000 | **$58** |
| Reflection of His Love 522279, 1990 | General Line | RT | **$50** |
| Reflection of His Love 529095, 1994 | Annual Eggs | YR | **$29** |
| Rejoice In Victory 283541, 1997 | Collectors' Club | CL | **$50** |
| Rejoice O Earth 520268, 1988 | Mini Nativity | OP | **$27** |
| Rejoice O Earth 617334, 1990 | Tree Topper | OP | **$140** |
| Rejoice O Earth E5636, 1984+ | Nativity | RT | **$35** |
| Rejoice O Earth E5636 (Fish Mark), 1983 | Nativity | RT | **$45** |
| Rejoice O Earth E5636 (Hourglass Mark), 1982 | Nativity | RT | **$65** |
| Rejoice O Earth E5636 (Triangle Mark), 1981 | Nativity | RT | **$70** |

The Purr-Fect Grandma E3109, 1980, **$35-$75.**

Put On a Happy
Face PM822,
Precious
Moments
Collectors' Club,
1982, **$145-$180.**

The Road to a Friend is Never Long C0024, Precious
Moments Collectors' Club, 2003, **$32.**

| Title | Series | Limit | Trend |
|-------|--------|-------|-------|
| Rejoice O Earth E5645, 1980 | Musical | RT | **$79** |
| Rejoicing In God's Gift of You 4003174, 2005 | General Line | OP | **$32** |
| Rejoicing With You E4724, 1980 | General Line | OP | **$65** |
| Rejoicing With You E4724, 1983+ | General Line | OP | **$55** |
| Rejoicing With You E4724 (Hourglass Mark), 1982 | General Line | OP | **$60** |
| Rejoicing With You E4724 (Triangle Mark), 1981 | General Line | OP | **$60** |
| Remember to Reach For the Stars 110263, 2003 | Animal Affections | OP | **$18** |
| Remember, We're In It Together 117800, 2004 | General Line | OP | **$45** |
| Renew Faith, Restore Hope, Replenish Love 4001784, 2005 | Century Circle Carousel | 2000 | **$68** |
| Rhythm and Flute (5 pieces) 791091, 2002 | Girl's Festival | OP | **$80** |
| Ring Around the Rosie waterball 868221, 2001 | General Line | CL | **$60** |
| Ring Out the Good News 529966, 1993 | Nativity | RT | **$31** |

| Title | Series | Limit | Trend |
|---|---|---|---|
| Ring Those Christmas Bells 525898, 1992 | General Line | RT | **$119** |
| Ringbearer E2833, 1984 | Bridal Party | RT | **$26** |
| Ringing In the Season 610001, 2006 | General Line | YR | **$35** |
| Road to a Friend Is Never Long, The C0024, 2003 | Collectors' Club | * | **$32** |
| Rock Around the Clock 710027, 2007 | General Line | 3,000 | **$80** |
| Roll Way, Roll Away, Roll Away 879002, 2001 | Special Wishes | OP | **$32** |
| Rose Beautiful, June 101521, 2002 | Calendar Girl | OP | **$36** |
| Royal Budge Is Good For the Soul, The 878987, 2001 | Nativity | OP | **$40** |
| Ruby—Color of Joy 335606, 1998 | Birthstone | OP | **$25** |
| Ruth and Naomi 649961, 2001 | Little Moments Bible Stories | OP | **$25** |
| RV Haven' Fun Or What 587915, 1999 | Special Wishes | RT | **$30** |
| Safe In the Arms of Jesus 521922, 1992 | General Line | OP | **$35** |

| Title | Series | Limit | Trend |
|---|---|---|---|
| Safe In the Hands of Love PM0032, 2003 | Collectors' Club | * | **$49** |
| Safely Home 120114, 2004 | General Line | OP | **$36** |
| Said the Little Lamb to the Shepherd Boy 610041, 2006 | General Line | CL | **$27** |
| Sailabration 150061, 1995 | General Line | YR | **$498** |
| Sam Butcher Sign 529567, 1992 | Sugar Town | YR | **$160** |
| Sam Butcher Sign 529842, 1993 | Sugar Town | YR | **$45** |
| Same Today, Yesterday and Forever, The 4004373, 2005 | General Line | OP | **$32** |
| Sammy 528668, 1992 | Sugar Town | RT | **$18** |
| Sammy 529222, 1993 | Sammy's Circus | SU | **$26** |
| Sam's House Collectors Set 531774, 1993 | Sugar Town | RT | **$217** |
| Sam's House nightlight 529605, 1993 | Sugar Town | RT | **$57** |
| Sapphire—Color of Confidence September 335622, 1998 | Birthstone | OP | **$25** |
| Saturday's Child Works Hard For a Living 692131, 2001 | Days of the Week | OP | **$20** |

| Title | Series | Limit | Trend |
|---|---|---|---|
| Say I Do 261149, 1997 | General Line | OP | **$53** |
| Scatter Joy 4024087, 2005 | General Line | OP | **$45** |
| Scent From Above 100528, 1987 | General Line | RT | **$32** |
| Schoolhouse Collectors Set 272876, 1997 | Sugar Town | RT | **$220** |
| Scoopin' Up Some Love 635049, 2000 | Events | RT | **$24** |
| Scootin' By Just to Say Hi! B0011, 1997 | Birthday Club | CL | **$21** |
| Scootin' By Just to Say Hi! B0111, 1997 | Birthday Club | CL | **$23** |
| Scootin' Your Way to a Perfect Day 634999, 1999 | Care-A-Van | RT | **$29** |
| Sealed With a Kiss 524441, 1993 | General Line | RT | **$55** |
| Seek and Ye Shall Find E0005, 1985 | Collectors' Club | CL | **$32** |
| Seek and Ye Shall Find E0105, 1985 | Collectors' Club | CL | **$38** |
| Seek Ye the Lord E9261, 1984-1986 | General Line | SU | **$40** |
| Seek Ye the Lord E9261 (Fish Mark), 1983 | General Line | SU | **$40** |

Sealed With a Kiss 524441, 1993, **$55.**

| Title | Series | Limit | Trend |
|---|---|---|---|
| Seek Ye the Lord E9262, 1984-1986 | General Line | SU | **$50** |
| Seek Ye the Lord E9262 (Fish Mark), 1983 | General Line | SU | **$60** |
| Seguro En Los Brazos De Padrinos 928453, 2001 | General Line | OP | **$45** |
| Sending My Love 100056, 1986 | General Line | SU | **$37** |
| Sending My Love Your Way 528609, 1995 | General Line | CL | **$37** |
| Sending You a Rainbow E9288 (Cross Mark), 1984 | Heavenly Halos | SU | **$85** |
| Sending You a Rainbow E9288 (Fish Mark), 1983 | Heavenly Halos | SU | **$90** |
| Sending You My Love 109967, 1988 | General Line | RT | **$60** |
| Sending You Oceans of Love 532010, 1995 | General Line | RT | **$38** |
| Sending You Showers of Blessings 520683, 1988 | General Line | RT | **$44** |
| September 110086, 1988 | Calendar Girl | RT | **$43** |
| September 261238, 1996 | Little Moments Birthstone Collection | OP | **$20** |

| Title | Series | Limit | Trend |
|---|---|---|---|
| September Girl With Water-ball 844365, 2001 | General Line | OP | **$30** |
| Serenity Prayer (Boy) 530700, 1994 | General Line | RT | **$27** |
| Serenity Prayer (Girl) 530697, 1994 | General Line | RT | **$36** |
| Serving the Lord 100161, 1985 | General Line | SU | **$32** |
| Serving the Lord 100293, 1985 | General Line | SU | **$31** |
| Serving Up Fun 104803, 2002 | Special Wishes | OP | **$23** |
| Sew In Love 106844, 1988 | General Line | RT | **$60** |
| Sharing a Gift of Love 527114, 1991 | Easter Seals | YR | **$40** |
| Sharing Begins In the Heart 520861, 1988 | Events | SU | **$29** |
| Sharing Fun and Games Together 120123, 2004 | Boys & Girls Clubs of America | YR | **$72** |
| Sharing Is Universal E0007, 1987 | Collectors' Club | CL | **$29** |
| Sharing Is Universal E0107, 1987 | Collectors' Club | CL | **$34** |

Seek and Ye
Shall Find
E0105, 1985,
**$38.**

Sending
My Love
100056,
1986, **$37.**

Sending You My Love 109967, 1988, **$60.**

Sew in Love 106844, 1988, **$60.**

| Title | Series | Limit | Trend |
|---|---|---|---|
| Sharing Our Christmas Together 102490, 1986 | Family Christmas | SU | **$54** |
| Sharing Our Christmas Together 524115, 2004 | General Line | OP | **$130** |
| Sharing Our Christmas Together 531944, 1994 | General Line | RT | **$23** |
| Sharing Our Joy Together E2834, 1982 | Bridal Party | SU | **$34** |
| Sharing Our Season Together E0501, 1983 | General Line | SU | **$116** |
| Sharing Our Season Together E0519 (Cross Mark), 1984 | Musical | RT | **$170** |
| Sharing Our Season Together E0519 (Fish Mark), 1983 | Musical | RT | **$150** |
| Sharing Our Time Is So Precious 456349, 1999 | Century Circle | CL | **$110** |
| Sharing Our Winter Wonderland 539988, 1999 | General Line | CL | **$75** |
| Sharing PM942, 1994 | Collectors' Club | CL | **$33** |
| Sharing Sweet Moments Together 526487, 1994 | General Line | RT | **$30** |
| Sharing Sweet Moments Together 731579, 2000 | Little Moments | CL | **$24** |

| Title | Series | Limit | Trend |
|---|---|---|---|
| Sharing the Gift of 40 Precious Years 163821, 1996 | To Have & to Hold | OP | **$56** |
| Sharing the Good News Together C0011, 1991 | Collectors' Club | CL | **$31** |
| Sharing the Good News Together C0111, 1991 | Collectors' Club | CL | **$32** |
| Sharing the Light of Love 272531, 1997 | General Line | RT | **$30** |
| Sharing the Season With You 702862, 2001 | Little Moments | OP | **$18** |
| Shear Happiness and Hare Cuts 539910, 1999 | Country Lane | RT | **$50** |
| Sheep 530077, 1993 | Noah's Ark/ Two By Two | RT | **$16** |
| Sheep, Bunny, Turtle 102296, 1986 | General Line | SU | **$39** |
| Shepherd of Love 102261, 1985 | Mini Nativity | OP | **$17** |
| Shepherd With Lambs set of 3 183954, 1997 | Nativity | OP | **$30** |
| Shepherd With Lambs set of 3 183962, 1997 | Nativity | OP | **$35** |
| Shepherd With Sheep set of 2 213616, 1997 | Mini Nativity | SU | **$40** |

Sharing the Season With You 702862, Little Moments, 2001, **$18.**

| Title | Series | Limit | Trend |
|---|---|---|---|
| Shiny New and Ready For School (Boy) 481637, 1999 | Special Wishes | CL | **$20** |
| Shiny New and Ready For School (Girl) 481629, 1999 | Special Wishes | CL | **$20** |
| Shoot For the Stars and You'll Never Strike Out 521701, 1997 | Boys & Girls Clubs of America | LE | **$39** |
| Showers of Blessings 105945, 1986 | Birthday Series | RT | **$17** |
| Sidewalk 533157, 1994 | Sugar Town | RT | **$15** |
| Silent Knight E5642, 1980 | Musical | SU | **$168** |
| Silent Knight E5642 (Cross Mark), 1984 | Musical | SU | **$410** |
| Silent Knight E5642 (Fish Mark), 1983 | Musical | SU | **$420** |
| Silent Knight E5642 (Hourglass Mark), 1982 | Musical | SU | **$435** |
| Silent Knight E5642 (Triangle Mark), 1981 | Musical | SU | **$470** |
| Silent Night 15814, 1985 | Family Christmas | SU | **$27** |
| Silver Celebration to Share, A 163813, 1996 | To Have and to Hold | OP | **$65** |

Sharing is Universal E0007, Precious Moments Collectors' Club,
1987, **$29.**

Sharing Our Season Together E0501, 1983, **$116.**

Sharing Sweet Moments Together 526487, 1994, **$30.**

| Title | Series | Limit | Trend |
|-------|--------|-------|-------|
| Simple Joys Put a Song In Your Heart 117794, 2004 | Hark the Heavens | 10,000 | **$40** |
| Simple Pleasures Are Life's Treasures 108542, 2003 | General Line | LE | **$75** |
| Simple Pleasures Make Holiday Treasures (set of 5) 111898, 2003 | General Line | RT | **$112** |
| Sing In Excelsis Deo 183830, 1996 | General Line | RT | **$130** |
| Sing Songs of Praise to Him 4003176, 2005 | General Line | 5000 | **$108** |
| Single Tree 533173, 1994 | Sugar Town | RT | **$14** |
| Sister Is a Gift to the Heart and a Friend, A 640032, 2007 | General Line | OP | **$55** |
| Sisters In Purple We'll Always Be 119435, 2004 | General Line | OP | **$36** |
| Sitting Pretty 104825, 1986 | General Line | SU | **$43** |
| Sixteen-Sweet! 115920, 2004 | General Line | OP | **$34** |
| Skating Pond 184047, 1996 | Sugar Town | RT | **$53** |
| Skating Sign 184020, 1996 | Sugar Town | YR | **$17** |
| Sleeping Baby Boy 429570, 1991 | Musical | OP | **$70** |

| Title | Series | Limit | Trend |
|---|---|---|---|
| Sleeping Baby Girl 429589, 1991 | Musical | OP | **$70** |
| Sleigh Bells Ring 610012, 2006 | General Line | * | **$60** |
| Slide Into the Celebration BC981, 1998 | Birthday Club | CL | **$17** |
| Slide Into the Next Millennium With Joy 587761, 1999 | Christmas Annual | CL | **$35** |
| Sliding Into the Season 775363, 2000 | General Line | OP | **$30** |
| Smile Along the Way 101842, 1987+ | General Line | RT | **$130** |
| Smile Along the Way 101842 (Olive Branch Mark), 1986 | General Line | RT | **$160** |
| Smile Is Cherished In the Heart, A 103177, 2002 | Rose Petals Series/ GoCollect Exclusive | CL | **$50** |
| Smile, God Loves You E1373B, 1979 | General Line | RT | **$95** |
| Smile, God Loves You E1373B, 1980 | General Line | RT | **$95** |
| Smile, God Loves You E1373B (Cross Mark), 1984 | General Line | RT | **$40** |
| Smile, God Loves You E1373B (Fish Mark), 1983 | General Line | RT | **$45** |

Silent Night 15814, Family Christmas series, 1985, **$27.**

Sisters in Purple We'll Always Be 119435, 2004, **$36.**

Sliding Into the Season 775363, 2000, **$30.**

Smile Along the Way 101842, 1986, **$130-$160.**

Smile, God Loves You E1373B, 1979, one of the Original 21 figurines, **$40-$95.**

| Title | Series | Limit | Trend |
|---|---|---|---|
| Smile, God Loves You E1373B (Hourglass Mark), 1982 | General Line | RT | **$55** |
| Smile, God Loves You E1373B (Triangle Mark), 1981 | General Line | RT | **$65** |
| Smile, God Loves You PM821 (Fish Mark), 1983 | Collectors' Club | CL | **$160** |
| Smile, God Loves You PM821 (Hourglass Mark, Members Only), 1982 | Collectors' Club | CL | **$175** |
| Smile, God Loves You PM821 (No Mark), 1982 | Collectors' Club | CL | **$280** |
| Smile's the Cymbal of Joy B0002, 1987 | Birthday Club | CL | **$44** |
| Smile's the Cymbal of Joy B0102, 1987 | Birthday Club | CL | **$50** |
| S'mitten With the Christmas Spirit 117785, 2004 | General Line | YR | **$32** |
| S'more Time Spent With You 4001647, 2005 | General Line | OP | **$49** |
| Snow Man Like My Man 587877, 1999 | General Line | SU | **$55** |
| Snowbunny Loves You Like I Do 183792, 1996 | General Line | RT | **$20** |
| Snowdrop Pure and Gentle, January 101515, 2002 | Calendar Girl | OP | **$36** |

A Smile's the Cymbal of Joy B0002, Precious Moments Birthday
Club, 1987, **$44.**

S'mitten With the Christmas Spirit 117785, 2004, **$32.**

Some Bunny's Sleeping 522996, Mini Nativity series, 1990, **$32.**

| Title | Series | Limit | Trend |
|-------|--------|-------|-------|
| Snowman Christmas Tree 4003323, 2005 | General Line | OP | **$43** |
| Snowman Holding Lantern 4003324, 2005 | General Line | OP | **$32** |
| Snowman Holding Wreath 4003325, 2005 | General Line | OP | **$33** |
| Snowman In Top Hat Street Light 4003322, 2005 | General Line | OP | **$43** |
| So Glad I Picked You As a Friend 524379, 1994 | General Line | YR | **$35** |
| So You Finally Met Your Match—Congratulations 101493, 2002 | Animal Affections | OP | **$18** |
| Soap Bubbles, Soap Bubbles 490342, 1999 | Little Moments | OP | **$35** |
| Some Bunny's Sleeping 115274, 1988 | Nativity | SU | **$19** |
| Some Bunny's Sleeping 522996, 1990 | Mini Nativity | SU | **$32** |
| Some Day My Prince Will Come 610056, 2006 | General Line | OP | **$40** |
| Some Plant, Some Water, But God Giveth the Increase 176958, 1996 | Growing In God's Garden of Love | OP | **$25** |
| Somebody Cares 522325, 1998 | Easter Seals | CL | **$28** |

| Title | Series | Limit | Trend |
|---|---|---|---|
| Somebunny Cares BC881, 1988 | Birthday Club | CL | **$43** |
| Some-bunny Loves You 4001247, 2004 | General Line | OP | **$45** |
| Someday My Love 520799, 1988 | General Line | RT | **$47** |
| Someday My Prince Will Come 610056, 2006 | General Line | OP | **$36** |
| Something Precious From Above 524360, 1997 | General Line | OP | **$86** |
| Something's Missing When You're Not Around 105643, 1988 | General Line | SU | **$55** |
| Sometimes You're Next to Impossible 530964, 1997 | General Line | OP | **$44** |
| Soot Yourself to a Merry Christmas 150096, 1995 | General Line | RT | **$26** |
| Sow Love to Grow Love 630007, 2007 | General Line | OP | **$30** |
| Sower and the Seed, The 650005, 2001 | Little Moments Bible Stories | OP | **$20** |
| Sowing Seeds of Kindness 163856, 1995 | Growing In God's Garden of Love | RT | **$26** |
| Sowing the Seeds of Love PM922, 1992 | Collectors' Club | CL | **$31** |

Somebody Cares 522325, Easter Seals, 1998, **$28.**

Something Precious From Above 524360, 1997, **$86.**

| Title | Series | Limit | Trend |
|---|---|---|---|
| Special Chime For Jesus, A 524468, 1992 | General Line | RT | **$26** |
| Special Delivery, A 521493, 1991 | General Line | OP | **$31** |
| Special Moment Just For You, A 115923, 2004 | Century Circle | LE | **$40** |
| Special Toast to Precious Moments, A C0017, 1997 | Collectors' Club | CL | **$25** |
| Special Toast to Precious Moments, A C0117, 1997 | Collectors' Club | CL | **$65** |
| Spirit Is Willing But the Flesh Is Weak, The 100196, 1987 | General Line | RT | **$53** |
| Sprinkled In Sweetness 4003182, 2005 | General Line | OP | **$54** |
| Sprinkled With Kindness 115927, 2004 | Special Wishes | LE | **$38** |
| Squashed With Love 112874, 2003 | General Line | OP | **$45** |
| Squeaky Clean 731048, 2000 | Century Circle | CL | **$62** |
| Stand Beside Her and Guide Her 106671, 2001 | America Forever | RT | **$40** |
| Standing In the Presence of the Lord 163732, 1996 | Dated Cross | SU | **$36** |

Sometimes You're Next to
Impossible 530964, 1997, **$44.**

Soot Yourself to a Merry
Christmas 150096, 1995,
**$26.**

Sow Love to Grow Love
630007, 2007, **$30.**

A Special Delivery 521493,
1991, **$31.**

The Spirit is Willing, But
the Flesh is Weak 100196,
1987, **$53.**

Stand Beside Her and
Guide Her 106671, America
Forever series, 2001, **$40.**

The Story of God's Love 15784,
Family Christmas, 1985, **$18.**

Summer's Joy 12076, Four
Seasons series, 1985, **$89.**

| Title | Series | Limit | Trend |
|---|---|---|---|
| Star of Wonder 4003169, 2005 | General Line | OP | **$40** |
| Stay With Me A-whale 108595, 2003 | Endangered Species | 7500 | **$45** |
| Stockings Were Hung By the Chimney With Care, The 710037, 2007 | Disney | OP | **$56** |
| Stork 529788, 1994 | Sugar Town | YR | **$27** |
| Story of God's Love, The 15784, 1985 | Family Christmas | SU | **$18** |
| Street Sign 532185, 1995 | Sugar Town | RT | **$15** |
| Stressed Is Desserts Spelled Backwards 120112, 2005 | Special Wishes | OP | **$28** |
| Sugar and Her Doghouse 533165, 1994 | Sugar Town | RT | **$20** |
| Sugar Town Accessories 212725, 1997 | Sugar Town | RT | **$35** |
| Sugar Town Enhancement Set 152269, 1995 | Sugar Town | RT | **$51** |
| Sugar Town Enhancement Set 184160, 1996 | Sugar Town | RT | **$45** |
| Sugar Town Enhancement Set 273015, 1997 | Sugar Town | RT | **$51** |
| Sugar Town Post Office Set 456217, 1998 | Sugar Town | YR | **$275** |

| Title | Series | Limit | Trend |
|---|---|---|---|
| Sugar Town School Set 272930, 1997 | Sugar Town | RT | **$190** |
| Sugar Town Set 184187, 1996 | Sugar Town | RT | **$190** |
| Sugar Town Skating Pond Set 184128 7-pcs., 1997 | Sugar Town | RT | **$208** |
| Sugar Town Train 152595, 1995 | Sugar Town | RT | **$85** |
| Sugar Town Train Station Set 184179, 1996 | Sugar Town | RT | **$189** |
| Sugar Town Train Station/Collectors Set 150193, 1995 | Sugar Town | RT | **$209** |
| Summer's Joy 12076, 1985 | Four Seasons | YR | **$89** |
| Summer's Joy Musical 408743, 1984 | Four Seasons | LE | **$178** |
| Sun Is Always Shining Somewhere, The 163775, 1996 | General Line | RT | **$27** |
| Sunday's Child Born On the Sabbath Day 692077, 2001 | Days of the Week | OP | **$20** |
| Sunshine Brings You a Purr-fect Friend PM386, 2004 | Pretty As a Princess | 10,000 | **$34** |
| Sure Could Use Less Hustle and Bustle 737550, 2000 | Christmas Remembered | OP | **$28** |

| Title | Series | Limit | Trend |
|---|---|---|---|
| Sure Would Love to Squeeze You (Germany) 456896, 1998 | Little Moments International | OP | **$27** |
| Surely Goodness and Mercy Shall Follow Me 523410 | Chapel Exclusive | * | **$29** |
| Surrounded With Joy 531677, 1993 | Chapel Exclusive | OP | **$37** |
| Surrounded With Joy 531685, 1993 | General Line | OP | **$31** |
| Surrounded With Joy E0506 (Cross Mark), 1984 | General Line | RT | **$65** |
| Surrounded With Joy E0506 (Fish Mark), 1983 | General Line | RT | **$85** |
| Sweep All Your Worries Away 521779 (Bow & Arrow Mark), 1989 | General Line | RT | **$95** |
| Sweep All Your Worries Away 521779 (Flame Mark), 1990 | General Line | RT | **$55** |
| Sweet Is the Voice of My Sister 640033, 2007 | General Line | OP | **$60** |
| Sweeter As the Years Go By 522333, 1996 | General Line | RT | **$64** |
| Sweetest Baby Boy 101500, 2002 | General Line | OP | **$18** |

| Title | Series | Limit | Trend |
|---|---|---|---|
| Sweetest Baby Girl 101501, 2002 | General Line | OP | **$18** |
| Sweetest Club Around, The B0003, 1988 | Birthday Club | CL | **$27** |
| Sweetest Club Around, The B0103, 1988 | Birthday Club | CL | **$23** |
| Sweetest Treat Is Friendship, The 110855, 2003 | Collectors' Club | * | **$55** |
| Tail of Love, A 679976, 2000 | Noah's Ark/ Two By Two | OP | **$80** |
| Take a Note, You're Great 112858, 2003 | Special Wishes | OP | **$27** |
| Take Heed When You Stand 521272, 1990 | General Line | SU | **$40** |
| Take It to the Lord In Prayer 163767, 1996 | General Line | RT | **$23** |
| Take My Hand 119460, 2004 | Ronald Mcdonald | LE | **$36** |
| Take Thyme For Yourself 731064, 2001 | General Line | SU | **$30** |
| Take Time For Your Birthday 488003, 1999 | Birthday Train | OP | **$25** |
| Take Time to Smell the Flowers 524387, 1995 | Easter Seals | SU | **$25** |
| Take Time to Smell the Roses 634980C, 1999 | General Line | OP | **$36** |

The Sun is Always Shining Somewhere 163775, 1996, **$27.**

Sunshine Brings You a Purr-fect Friend PM386, Pretty As a Princess series, 2004, **$34.**

Sweep All Your Worries Away 521779, 1990, **$55-$95.**

The Sweetest Club Around
B0003, Precious Moments
Birthday Club, 1988, **$27.**

Teddy E9267A, Animal
Collection, 1988, **$15.**

Tell Me a Story 15792,
Family Christmas series,
1985, **$21.**

Thank You for Coming to My
Ade E5202, 1981, **$90-$105.**

| Title | Series | Limit | Trend |
|---|---|---|---|
| Tassel Was No Hassle, The 4001812, 2005 | General Line | OP | **$36** |
| Taste and See That the Lord Is Good E9274, 1984-1986 | Heavenly Halos | RT | **$63** |
| Taste and See That the Lord Is Good E9274 (Fish Mark), 1983 | Heavenly Halos | RT | **$70** |
| Teach Us to Love One Another 211672, 1996 | Collectors' Club | * | **$10** |
| Teach Us to Love One Another PM961, 1996 | Collectors' Club | CL | **$49** |
| Teacher, You're a Precious Work of Art 112861, 2003 | Special Wishes | RT | **$27** |
| Teddy E9267A, 1988 | Animal Collection | SU | **$15** |
| Tell It to Jesus 521477, 1988 | General Line | RT | **$40** |
| Tell Me a Story 15792, 1985 | Family Christmas | SU | **$21** |
| Tell Me the Story of Jesus E2349, 1982 | General Line | SU | **$77** |
| Ten Wonderful Years of Wishes BC952, 1995 | Birthday Club | CL | **$52** |
| Ten Years and Still Going Strong PM901, 1990 | Collectors' Club | CL | **$32** |

| Title | Series | Limit | Trend |
|-------|--------|-------|-------|
| Ten Years Heart to Heart 163805, 1996 | To Have and To Hold | OP | **$65** |
| Tender Touch Helps Love Bloom, A 630006, 2007 | General Line | OP | **$40** |
| Thank You For Coming to My Ade E5202 (Cross Mark), 1984 | General Line | SU | **$90** |
| Thank You For Coming to My Ade E5202 (Fish Mark), 1983 | General Line | SU | **$90** |
| Thank You For Coming to My Ade E5202 (Hourglass Mark), 1982 | General Line | SU | **$95** |
| Thank You For Coming to My Ade E5202 (Triangle Mark), 1981 | General Line | SU | **$105** |
| Thank You For the Time We Share 384836, 1998 | Little Moments | RT | **$25** |
| Thank You For Your Membership 5 Years 635243, 2000 | Collectors' Club | CL | **$31** |
| Thank You Lord For Everything 522031, 1988 | General Line | SU | **$80** |
| Thank You Sew Much 587923, 1999 | Special Wishes | OP | **$22** |

| Title | Series | Limit | Trend |
|---|---|---|---|
| Thankful For My Family 4003166, 2005 | General Line | OP | **$63** |
| Thanking Him For You E7155 (Cross Mark), 1984 | General Line | SU | **$45** |
| Thanking Him For You E7155 (Fish Mark), 1983 | General Line | SU | **$50** |
| Thanking Him For You E7155 (Hourglass Mark), 1982 | General Line | SU | **$60** |
| Thanks a Bunch C0020, 2000 | Collectors' Club | CL | **$29** |
| Thanks a Bunch C0120, 2000 | Collectors' Club | CL | **$33** |
| Thanks For a Quarter Century of Loving, Caring and Sharing 108602, 2003 | 25th Anniversary | LE | **$90** |
| That's What Friends Are For 521183, 1989 | General Line | RT | **$58** |
| Thee I Love E3116, 1980 | General Line | RT | **$140** |
| Thee I Love E3116, 1984+ | General Line | RT | **$65** |
| Thee I Love E3116 (Fish Mark), 1983 | General Line | RT | **$80** |
| Thee I Love E3116 (Hourglass Mark), 1982 | General Line | RT | **$85** |

| Title | Series | Limit | Trend |
|---|---|---|---|
| Thee I Love E3116 (Triangle Mark), 1981 | General Line | RT | **$85** |
| There Are Two Sides to Every Story 325368, 1998 | General Line | RT | **$17** |
| There Is Joy In Serving Jesus E7157, 1984-1986 | General Line | RT | **$35** |
| There Is Joy In Serving Jesus E7157 (Fish Mark), 1983 | General Line | RT | **$45** |
| There Is Joy In Serving Jesus E7157 (Hourglass Mark), 1982 | General Line | RT | **$55** |
| There Is No Greater Treasure Than to Have a Friend Like You 521000, 1993 | General Line | RT | **$31** |
| There Shall Be Showers of Blessings 522090, 1989 | General Line | RT | **$73** |
| There's a Light At the End of the Tunnel 521485, 1990 | General Line | SU | **$50** |
| There's a Song In My Heart 12173, 1984 | Rejoice In the Lord | SU | **$39** |
| There's a Spot In My Heart For You BC961, 1996 | Birthday Club | CL | **$23** |
| There's Always a Place In My Heart For You C0023, 2003 | Collectors' Club | * | **$29** |

Tis the Season 111163, 1988, **$24.**

Thee I Love E3116, 1980, **$65-$140.**

There is No Greater Treasure Than to Have a Friend Like You 521000, 1993, **$31.**

There's Sno-Boredom With You 730122, 2000, **$40.**

They Followed the Star three-piece set 108243, Mini Nativity series, 1987, **$130.**

| Title | Series | Limit | Trend |
|---|---|---|---|
| There's Always a Place In My Heart For You C0123, 2003 | Collectors' Club | * | **$35** |
| There's More to Life Than Nine to Five 120107, 2004 | General Line | OP | **$36** |
| There's No Place Like Home For Christmas 4003172, 2005 | General Line | OP | **$35** |
| There's No Wrong Way With You 649473, 2001 | Little Moments Signs of Guidance | OP | **$16** |
| There's Nothin' to It When It Comes to You 710038, 2007 | Disney | OP | **$52** |
| There's Sno-Boredom With You 730122, 2000 | General Line | OP | **$40** |
| There's Sno-One Quite Like You 104781, 2002 | Little Moments | OP | **$29** |
| There's Snow Place Like Home 118129, 2004 | General Line | LE | **$36** |
| They Call It Puppy Love 630012, 2006 | General Line | OP | **$40** |
| They Followed the Star 108243, 1987 | Mini Nativity | SU | **$130** |
| They Followed the Star E5624, 1980 | Nativity | OP | **$320** |

| Title | Series | Limit | Trend |
|---|---|---|---|
| They Followed the Star E5624, 1983+ | Nativity | OP | **$225-$245** |
| They Followed the Star E5624 (Hourglass Mark), 1982 | Nativity | OP | **$275** |
| They Followed the Star E5624 (Triangle Mark), 1981 | Nativity | OP | **$290** |
| They Followed the Star E5641, 1980 | Nativity | SU | **$169** |
| Things Are Poppin' At Our House This Christmas 455806, 2000 | General Line | OP | **$40** |
| Thinking of You Is What I Really Like to Do 522287, 1989 | General Line | SU | **$28** |
| This Bears My Love For You (Boy) 4024083, 2005 | General Line | OP | **$32** |
| This Bears My Love For You (Girl) 4004371, 2005 | General Line | OP | **$35** |
| This Day Has Been Made In Heaven 523496, 1989 | General Line | OP | **$30** |
| This Day Has Been Made In Heaven 523682, 1992 | Musical | RT | **$57** |
| This Day Has Been Made In Heaven 679852, 2000 | General Line | OP | **$27** |

| Title | Series | Limit | Trend |
|---|---|---|---|
| This Day Is Something to Roar About 15989, 1985 | Birthday Train | OP | **$23** |
| This Is the Day the Lord Hath Made 12157, 1986 | General Line | SU | **$28** |
| This Is the Day the Lord Hath Made E2838, 1987 | Bridal Party | SU | **$205** |
| This Is Your Day to Shine E2822, 1983 | General Line | RT | **$135** |
| This Land Is Our Land 527386, 1992 | Collectors' Club | CL | **$345** |
| This Land Is Our Land 527777, 1992 | General Line | CL | **$27** |
| This Little Light of Mine, I'm Gonna Let It Shine 113949, 2003 | General Line | OP | **$32** |
| This Too Shall Pass 114014, 1987 | General Line | RT | **$29** |
| Thou Art Mine E3113, 1980 | General Line | RT | **$70** |
| Thou Art Mine E3113, 1983+ | General Line | RT | **$40** |
| Thou Art Mine E3113 (Hourglass Mark), 1982 | General Line | RT | **$45** |
| Thou Art Mine E3113 (Triangle Mark), 1981 | General Line | RT | **$50** |

Thimble group: Mother Sew Dear, **$30**; Love Covers All, **$15**; God is Love, Dear Valentine, **$15**; and The Purr-fect Grandma, **$7**.

This Bears My Love for You 4004371, 2005, **$35.**

This Day is Something to Roar About 15989, Birthday Train, 1985, **$23.**

Thou Art Mine E3113, 1980, **$40-$70.**

Tied Up For the Holidays 527580, 1993, **$35.**

To a Special Dad E5212, 1981, **$30-$50.**

To a Very Special Mom E2824, 1984, **$12.**

| Title | Series | Limit | Trend |
|-------|--------|-------|-------|
| Thou Preparest a Table Before Me 523372, 1998 | Chapel Exclusive | 7500 | **$29** |
| Thoughts of You Are So Hearth Warming 4004377, 2005 | Catalog Exclusive | OP | **$48** |
| Thumb-body Loves You 521698, 1990 | General Line | SU | **$45** |
| Thursday's Child Has Far to Go 692115, 2001 | Days of the Week | OP | **$20** |
| Tidings of Comforter and Joy 117792, 2004 | Christmas Remembered | OP | **$45** |
| Tied Up For the Holidays 527580, 1993 | General Line | SU | **$35** |
| Til the End of Time (Just Married) 4001653, 2005 | General Line | OP | **$54** |
| Time For a Holy Holiday 455849, 1998 | General Line | RT | **$47** |
| Time Heals 523739, 1989 | General Line | RT | **$45** |
| Time to Wish You a Merry Christmas 115339, 1988 | Christmas Annual | CL | **$35** |
| Time to Wish You a Merry Christmas thimble 115312, 1988 | General Line | YR | **$29** |

| Title | Series | Limit | Trend |
|---|---|---|---|
| Time to Wish You a Merry Christmas, A 111895, 2004 | General Line | OP | **$45** |
| Tippy 529192, 1993 | Sammy's Circus | SU | **$13** |
| Tis the Season 111163, 1988 | General Line | SU | **$24** |
| To a Niece With a Bubbly Personality 112870, 2003 | General Line | OP | **$27** |
| To a Special Dad E5212, 1985+ | General Line | SU | **$30** |
| To a Special Dad E5212 (Cross Mark), 1984 | General Line | SU | **$35** |
| To a Special Dad E5212 (Fish Mark), 1983 | General Line | SU | **$40** |
| To a Special Dad E5212 (Hourglass Mark), 1982 | General Line | SU | **$45** |
| To a Special Dad E5212 (Triangle Mark), 1981 | General Line | SU | **$50** |
| To a Special Mum 521965, 1990 | General Line | RT | **$33** |
| To a Very Special Mom and Dad 521434, 1990 | General Line | SU | **$34** |
| To a Very Special Mom E2824, 1984 | General Line | RT | **$12** |
| To a Very Special Sister 528633, 1994 | General Line | RT | **$76** |

| Title | Series | Limit | Trend |
|---|---|---|---|
| To a Very Special Sister E2825, 1983 | General Line | RT | **$55** |
| To Be With You Is Uplifting 522260, 1988 | Birthday Series | RT | **$31** |
| To God Be the Glory (Blue Eyes) E2823R, 2000 | Events | RT | **$32** |
| To God Be the Glory E2823, 1983 | General Line | RT | **$66** |
| To Have and to Hold 630028, 2007 | Bluebirds of Happiness | OP | **$60** |
| To My Better Half 114016, 2003 | General Line | OP | **$35** |
| To My Deer Friend 100048, 1987 | General Line | RT | **$50** |
| To My Favorite Fan 521043, 1990 | Birthday Series | SU | **$25** |
| To My Favorite Paw 100021, 1986 | General Line | SU | **$78** |
| To My Forever Friend 100072, 1986 | General Line | OP | **$55** |
| To Some Bunny Special E9282A, 1988 | General Line | SU | **$30** |
| To Some Bunny Special E9282, 1983+ | General Line | SU | **$30** |
| To Some Bunny Special E9282 (Hourglass Mark), 1982 | General Line | SU | **$35** |

To My Better Half 114016,
2003, **$35.**

To My Deer Friend 100048,
1987, **$50.**

To My Favorite Paw 100021,
1986, **$78.**

To My Forever Friend
100072, 1986, **$55.**

| Title | Series | Limit | Trend |
|---|---|---|---|
| To Tell the Tooth You're Special 105813, 1986 | General Line | SU | **$210** |
| To the Apple of God's Eye 522015, 1992 | General Line | RT | **$36** |
| To the Sweetest Girl In the Cast 742880, 2001 | Special Wishes | OP | **$35** |
| To Thee With Love E3120, 1980 | General Line | SU | **$85** |
| To Thee With Love E3120, 1984-1986 | General Line | SU | **$50** |
| To Thee With Love E3120 (Fish Mark), 1983 | General Line | SU | **$55** |
| To Thee With Love E3120 (Hourglass Mark), 1982 | General Line | SU | **$60** |
| To Thee With Love E3120 (Triangle Mark), 1981 | General Line | SU | **$60** |
| Together Fur-Ever 108600, 2003 | Endangered Species | 7,500 | **$45** |
| Together Is the Nicest Place to Be 4003175, 2005 | General Line | OP | **$75** |
| Too Dog-Gone Sweet 0000387, 2004 | Pretty As a Princess | 10,000 | **$38** |
| Topaz—Color of Truth November 335665, 1998 | Calendar Girl | OP | **$25** |

| Title | Series | Limit | Trend |
|-------|--------|-------|-------|
| Tossing a Little Luck Your Way 120108, 2004 | Special Wishes | OP | **$35** |
| Train Cargo Car 273007, 1997 | Sugar Town | YR | **$32** |
| Train Station nightlight 150150, 1995 | Sugar Town | RT | **$97** |
| True Blue Friends BC912, 1991 | Birthday Club | CL | **$29** |
| True Friends Share One Heart 4003164, 2005 | General Line | OP | **$60** |
| True Spirit of Christmas Guides the Way, The 104784, 2002 | Events | 5,000 | **$100** |
| Trust In the Lord E9289, 1984-1987 | Heavenly Halos | SU | **$60** |
| Trust In the Lord E9289 (Fish Mark), 1983 | Heavenly Halos | SU | **$85** |
| Trust In the Lord E9289 (Hourglass Mark), 1982 | Heavenly Halos | SU | **$77** |
| Trust In the Lord to the Finish PM842, 1984 | Collectors' Club | CL | **$55** |
| Tub Full of Love, A 104817, 1987 | General Line | SU | **$34** |
| Tub Full of Love, A 112313, 1987 | General Line | SU | **$39** |
| Tubby's First Christmas 525278, 1992 | Mini Nativity | RT | **$13** |

To Thee With Love E3120,
1980, **$50-$85.**

Trust in the Lord to the Finish
PM842, Precious Moments
Collectors' Club, 1984, **$55.**

A Tub Full of Love 104817,
1987, **$34.**

A Tub Full of Love 112313,
1987, **$39.**

Tubby's First
Christmas
525278,
Mini Nativity
series,
1992, **$13.**

| Title | Series | Limit | Trend |
|-------|--------|-------|-------|
| Tubby's First Christmas E0511, 1983 | Nativity | SU | **$42** |
| Tuesday's Child Is Full of Grace 692093, 2001 | Days of the Week | OP | **$30** |
| Tuning Into Happy Times (1920s) 4001669, 2005 | Through the Years | 7,500 | **$50** |
| Turquoise—Color of Loyalty December 335673, 1998 | Birthstone | OP | **$25** |
| Twas the Night Before Christmas and All Through the House 117798, 2004 | General Line | YR | **$125** |

| Title | Series | Limit | Trend |
|---|---|---|---|
| Twinkle, Twinkle Little Star 729515, 2003 | Nursery Rhyme | OP | **$20** |
| Twinkle, Twinkle, You're a Star 0000384, 2004 | Pretty As a Princess | 10,000 | **$38** |
| Two Scoots Are Better When Shared With You 710032, 2007 | General Line | OP | **$45** |
| Twogether We Can Move Mountains 104276, 2002 | Boys & Girls Clubs of America | YR | **$80** |
| Un Dia Muy Especial 902098, 2001 | General Line | OP | **$30** |
| Una Bendicion Del Cielo 928488, 2001 | General Line | OP | **$40** |
| Una Madre Es El Corazon De La Familia 902101, 2001 | General Line | SU | **$30** |
| Universal Love, A 527173, 1992 | Easter Seals | CL | **$137** |
| Until We Meet Again 4003183, 2006 | Chapel Exclusive | OP | **$55** |
| Unto Us a Child Is Born E2013, 1979 | General Line | SU | **$120** |
| Unto Us a Child Is Born E2013, 1980-1981 | General Line | SU | **$130** |

| Title | Series | Limit | Trend |
|---|---|---|---|
| Unto Us a Child Is Born E2013 (Cross Mark), 1984 | General Line | SU | **$80** |
| Unto Us a Child Is Born E2013 (Fish Mark), 1983 | General Line | SU | **$90** |
| Unto Us a Child Is Born E2013 (Hourglass Mark), 1982 | General Line | SU | **$90** |
| Unto Us a Child Is Born E2808, 1980 | Musical | SU | **$145** |
| Unto Us a Child Is Born E2808 (Cross Mark), 1984 | Musical | SU | **$100** |
| Unto Us a Child Is Born E2808 (Fish Mark), 1983 | Musical | SU | **$105** |
| Unto Us a Child Is Born E2808 (Hourglass Mark), 1982 | Musical | SU | **$115** |
| Unto Us a Child Is Born E2808, 1980-1981 | Musical | SU | **$120** |
| Up to Our Ears In a White Christmas 879185, 2001 | General Line | CL | **$76** |
| Vaya Con Dios (Go With God) 531146, 1995 | General Line | RT | **$40** |
| Very Special Bond, A 488240, 1999 | General Line | OP | **$48** |
| Village Town Hall Clock 532908, 1994 | Sugar Town | RT | **$114** |

| Title | Series | Limit | Trend |
|---|---|---|---|
| Violet Modest, March 101518, 2002 | Calendar Girl | OP | **$36** |
| Visions of Sugarplums 610036, 2006 | General Line | OP | **$54** |
| Voice of Spring Musical, The 408735, 1984 | Four Seasons | LE | **$178** |
| Voice of Spring, The 12068, 1985 | Four Seasons | YR | **$140** |
| Waddle I Do Without You 12459, 1985 | Clown | RT | **$46** |
| Wait Patiently On the Lord 325279, 2001 | General Line | RT | **$20** |
| Waiting For a Merry Christmas 527637, 2000 | General Line | RT | **$65** |
| Walk In the Sonshine 524212, 1995 | General Line | RT | **$24** |
| Walk, Run, Empower 4001662, 2005 | General Line | OP | **$34** |
| Walking By Faith E3117, 1980 | General Line | RT | **$125** |
| Walking By Faith E3117, 1983+ | General Line | RT | **$90** |
| Walking By Faith E3117 (Hourglass Mark), 1982 | General Line | RT | **$100** |
| Walking By Faith E3117 (Triangle Mark), 1981 | General Line | RT | **$100** |

| Title | Series | Limit | Trend |
|---|---|---|---|
| Warmest Wishes For the Holidays 112881, 2003 | General Line | OP | **$45** |
| Warmest Wishes For the Holidays 455830, 1999 | General Line | RT | **$47** |
| Warmth of Christmas Comes From the Heart, The 690012, 2007 | General Line | OP | **$40** |
| Water I Do Without You 108547, 2003 | Sea of Friendship | OP | **$45** |
| Water-Melancholy Day Without You 521515, 1998 | Special Wishes | RT | **$38** |
| We All Have Our Bad Hair Days 261157, 1997 | Special Wishes | RT | **$58** |
| We All Need a Friend Through the Ruff Times 525901, 2002 | General Line | OP | **$40** |
| We Are All Precious In His Sight 102903, 1987 | General Line | YR | **$40** |
| We Are All Precious In His Sight 475068, 1999 | Easter Seals | CL | **$510** |
| We Are God's Workmanship 272434, 1997 | Baby Classics | RT | **$22** |
| We Are God's Workmanship 523879, 1991 | Easter Seals | CL | **$641** |
| We Are God's Workmanship 525960, 1992 | General Line | YR | **$27** |

| Title | Series | Limit | Trend |
|---|---|---|---|
| We Are God's Workmanship E9258, 1983+ | General Line | RT | **$35** |
| We Are God's Workmanship E9258 (Hourglass Mark), 1982 | General Line | RT | **$60** |
| We Belong to the Lord 103004, 1986 | General Line | SP | **$167** |
| We Fix Souls 4001574, 2005 | Premier Collection | 3,000 | **$135** |
| We Gather Together For Fun and Laughter 710048, 2007 | General Line | OP | **$16** |
| We Gather Together to Ask the Lord's Blessing 109762, 1986 | General Line | RT | **$300** |
| We Have Come From Afar 526959, 1990 | Nativity | SU | **$14** |
| We Have Come From Afar 530913, 1995 | Mini Nativity | RT | **$14** |
| We Have Seen His Star E2010, 1979 | Nativity | SU | **$135** |
| We Have Seen His Star E2010, 1980-1981 | Nativity | SU | **$105** |
| We Have Seen His Star E2010 (Cross Mark), 1984 | Nativity | SU | **$80** |
| We Have Seen His Star E2010 (Fish Mark), 1983 | Nativity | SU | **$80** |

A Very Special Bond
488240, 1999, **$48.**

Waddle I Do Without You
12459, Clown series, 1985, **$46.**

The Voice of Spring 12068, Four
Seasons series, 1985, **$140.**

We're Going to Miss You 524913, 1990, **$59.**

We're In It Together E9259, 1982, **$55.**

| Title | Series | Limit | Trend |
|---|---|---|---|
| We Have Seen His Star E2010 (Hourglass Mark), 1982 | Nativity | SU | **$85** |
| We Have the Sweetest Times Together 261580, 2001 | Century Circle | CL | **$100** |
| We Knead You, Grandma 679844, 2000 | General Line | OP | **$36** |
| We Need a Good Friend Through the Ruff Times 520810, 1989 | General Line | SU | **$36** |
| We Saw a Star 12408, 1984 | Musical | SU | **$110** |
| We Share a Love Forever Young—50th Anniversary 115912, 2004 | General Line | OP | **$45** |
| Wedding Arch 102369, 1987 | Bridal Party | SU | **$39** |
| Wednesday's Child Is Full of Woe 692107, 2001 | Days of the Week | OP | **$20** |
| Wee Three Kings 213624, 1996 | Mini Nativity | SU | **$55** |
| Wee Three Kings E0520, 1984+ | Musical | SU | **$135** |
| Wee Three Kings E0520 (Fish Mark), 1983 | Musical | SU | **$125** |
| Wee Three Kings E5635, 1983+ | Nativity | OP | **$85** |

| Title | Series | Limit | Trend |
|-------|--------|-------|-------|
| Wee Three Kings E5635 (Hourglass Mark), 1982 | Nativity | OP | **$90** |
| Wee Three Kings E5635 (Triangle Mark), 1981 | Nativity | OP | **$125** |
| Well, Blow Me Down It's Yer Birthday 325538, 1998 | General Line | RT | **$34** |
| We're a Family That Sticks Together 730114, 2000 | General Line | CL | **$40** |
| We're a Perfect Match 104801, 2002 | Special Wishes | OP | **$23** |
| We're Behind You All the Way 994863, 2002 | Animal Affections | OP | **$18** |
| We're Going to Miss You 524913, 1990 | General Line | RT | **$59** |
| We're In It Together E9259, 1982 | General Line | SU | **$55** |
| We're Pulling For You 106151, 1986 | General Line | SU | **$55** |
| We're So Hoppy You're Here 261351, 1997 | Events | SU | **$27** |
| We've Got the Wright Plan 937282, 2002 | Special Wishes | OP | **$80** |
| What a Difference You've Made In My Life 531138, 1996 | General Line | RT | **$49** |

| Title | Series | Limit | Trend |
|---|---|---|---|
| What Better to Give Than Yourself 487988, 1999 | General Line | RT | **$28** |
| What the World Needs Is Love 531065, 1995 | General Line | RT | **$33** |
| What the World Needs Now 524352, 1991 | General Line | RT | **$50** |
| What Would I Do Without You? 320714, 1997 | Little Moments | OP | **$22** |
| When They Saw the Star They Were Overjoyed 710040, 2007 | Nativity | OP | **$28** |
| Where the Deer and the Antelope Play 101552, 2002 | General Line | RT | **$35** |
| Where Would I Be Without You? 139491, 1996 | Little Moments | OP | **$18** |
| Whole Year Filled With Special Moments, A, First Anniversary 115910, 2004 | General Line | * | **$45** |
| Who's Gonna Fill Your Shoes (Boy) 532061S, 1997 | General Line | RT | **$34** |
| Who's Gonna Fill Your Shoes (Girl) 531634, 1997 | General Line | OP | **$38** |
| Who's Gonna Fill Your Shoes 532061, 1998 | General Line | RT | **$40** |
| Windows of Wonder—Boy and Clock 112421, 2003 | General Line | * | **$45** |

| Title | Series | Limit | Trend |
|-------|--------|-------|-------|
| Windows of Wonder—Girl and Tree 112420, 2003 | General Line | * | **$28** |
| Winning Spirit Comes From Within, A 813044, 2001 | General Line | OP | **$50** |
| Winter Wonderland Awaits, A 4001787, 2005 | Century Circle Carousel | 2,000 | **$75** |
| Winter's Song 12092, 1986 | Four Seasons | YR | **$119** |
| Winter's Song Musical 408778, 1984 | Four Seasons | LE | **$177** |
| Wise Men Still Seek Him 117791, 2004 | General Line | 7,500 | **$25** |
| Wish You Were Hare 110447, 2003 | Special Wishes | OP | **$36** |
| Wishes For the World 530018, 1999 | General Line | OP | **$39** |
| Wishing Well 292753, 1997 | Natvity | RT | **$24** |
| Wishing You a Basket Full of Blessings 109924, 1987 | General Line | RT | **$39** |
| Wishing You a Birthday Fit For a Princess 108534, 2003 | General Line | OP | **$23** |
| Wishing You a Birthday Full of Surprises 795313, 2001 | General Line | SU | **$40** |
| Wishing You a Comfy Christmas 527750, 1992 | Nativity | RT | **$31** |

What the World Needs is
Love 531065, 1995, **$33.**

What the World Needs Now
524352, 1991, **$50.**

Where Would I
Be Without You?
139491, Little
Moments, 1996,
**$18.**

Winter's Song 12092, Four Seasons series, 1986, **$119.**

Wish You Were Hare
110447, 2003, **$36.**

Wishes for the World
530018, 1999, **$39.**

Wishing You a Cozy Season
521949, 1989, **$38.**

Wishing You a Ho, Ho, Ho
527629, 1992, **$49.**

Wishing You a Season Filled With Joy E2805, 1980, **$80-$120.**

You Are a Precious Gift Precious Daughter 4001656, 2005, **$23.**

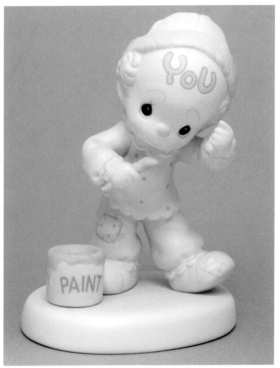

You Are Always on My Mind 306967, 1998, **$27.**

| Title | Series | Limit | Trend |
|-------|--------|-------|-------|
| Wishing You a Cozy Christmas 102342, 1985 | Christmas Annual | CL | **$33** |
| Wishing You a Cozy Christmas thimble 102334, 1986 | General Line | YR | **$17** |
| Wishing You a Cozy Season 521949, 1989 | General Line | SU | **$38** |
| Wishing You a Happy Bear Hug 520659, 1995 | Birthday Series | SU | **$22** |
| Wishing You a Happy Easter 109886, 1988 | General Line | RT | **$26** |
| Wishing You a Heavenly Holiday 118301, 2006 | General Line | OP | **$45** |
| Wishing You a Ho Ho Ho 117855, 2004 | General Line | OP | **$20** |
| Wishing You a Ho Ho Ho 527629, 1992 | General Line | RT | **$49** |
| Wishing You a Merry Christmas E5383, 1984 | Christmas Annual | CL | **$26** |
| Wishing You a Merry Christmas E5394, 1984 | Musical | SU | **$97** |
| Wishing You a Moo-ie Christmas 455865, 1999 | Country Lane | OP | **$60** |
| Wishing You a Perfect Choice 520845, 1988 | General Line | OP | **$65** |

| Title | Series | Limit | Trend |
|---|---|---|---|
| Wishing You a Season Filled With Joy E2805, 1980 | General Line | RT | **$120** |
| Wishing You a Season Filled With Joy E2805, 1984+ | General Line | RT | **$80** |
| Wishing You a Season Filled With Joy E2805 (Fish Mark), 1983 | General Line | RT | **$90** |
| Wishing You a Season Filled With Joy E2805, 1981-1982 | General Line | RT | **$100** |
| Wishing You a Very Successful Season 522120, 1989 | General Line | RT | **$54** |
| Wishing You a World of Peace C0019, 1999 | Collectors' Club | CL | **$25** |
| Wishing You a World of Peace C0119, 1999 | Collectors' Club | CL | **$41** |
| Wishing You a Year Filled With Birthday Cheer 630016, 2007 | General Line | OP | **$35** |
| Wishing You a Yummy Christmas 109754, 1986 | General Line | SU | **$36** |
| Wishing You a Yummy Christmas 455814, 1998 | General Line | RT | **$28** |
| Wishing You An Old Fashioned Christmas 634778, 1999 | Family Christmas | CL | **$180** |

| Title | Series | Limit | Trend |
|-------|--------|-------|-------|
| Wishing You Grr-eatness 109479, 1988 | Birthday Train | OP | **$20** |
| Wishing You Roads of Happiness 520780, 1988 | General Line | OP | **$73** |
| Wishing You the Sweetest Birthday 120113, 2004 | General Line | OP | **$32** |
| Wishing You the Sweetest Christmas 530166, 1993 | Christmas Annual | CL | **$39** |
| Wishing You the Sweetest Christmas thimble 530182, 1993 | General Line | OP | **$17** |
| Wishing You Were Here Musical 526916, 1993 | Musical | RT | **$97** |
| Witch Way Do You Spell Love? 587869, 1999 | General Line | RT | **$25** |
| With a Little Help From Above 111897, 2004 | Events | CL | **$45** |
| With This Ring... 104019, 1986 | General Line | OP | **$57** |
| Wonder of It All, The 710008, 2007 | General Line | OP | **$40** |
| Wonderful Thing About Tiggers, The 630037 | Disney Showcase Collection | OP | **$51** |
| Wooden Barrel Hot Cocoa Stand 184144, 1996 | Sugar Town | RT | **$18** |

| Title | Series | Limit | Trend |
|---|---|---|---|
| World of Possibilities Lies Ahead, A 640047, 2007 | General Line | OP | **$43** |
| World's Best Helper (Girl) 491608, 1999 | Little Moments | OP | **$18** |
| World's Greatest Student (Boy) 491586, 1999 | Little Moments | OP | **$18** |
| World's Greatest Student (Girl) 491616, 1999 | Little Moments | OP | **$20** |
| World's Sweetest Girl 491594, 1999 | Little Moments | OP | **$20** |
| Year of Blessings, A 163783, 1996 | To Have & to Hold | OP | **$65** |
| Yer a Pel-i-can Count On BC942, 1994 | Birthday Club | CL | **$27** |
| Yes, Dear, You're Always Right 523186, 2000 | Century Circle | RT | **$125** |
| Yield Not to Temptation 521310, 1989 | General Line | SU | **$28** |
| Yield to Him 649546, 2001 | Little Moments Signs of Guidance | OP | **$20** |
| You Add Sparkle to My Life 745413, 2001 | Care-A-Van | CL | **$25** |
| You Always Stand Behind Me 492140, 1999 | General Line | OP | **$44** |

| Title | Series | Limit | Trend |
|---|---|---|---|
| You Are a Blessing to Me PM902, 1990 | Collectors' Club | CL | **$35** |
| You Are a Child of God 4004681, 2005 | General Line | OP | **$23** |
| You Are a Child of God 4004880, 2005 | General Line | OP | **$30** |
| You Are a Dutch-ess to Me (Holland) 456373, 1998 | Little Moments International | OP | **$20** |
| You Are a Precious Gift 4001656, 2005 | General Line | * | **$23** |
| You Are a Real Cool Mommy 109495, 2002 | Animal Affections | OP | **$20** |
| You Are a Work of Art 640046, 2007 | General Line | OP | **$45** |
| You Are Always In My Heart (Boy) 768952, 2001 | Events | CL | **$51** |
| You Are Always In My Heart (Girl) 768987, 2001 | General Line | CL | **$51** |
| You Are Always On My Mind 306967, 1998 | General Line | RT | **$27** |
| You Are Always There For Me 163597, 1997 | General Line | RT | **$34** |
| You Are Always There For Me 163619, 1997 | General Line | OP | **$48** |

| Title | Series | Limit | Trend |
|---|---|---|---|
| You Are Always There For Me 163627, 1996 | General Line | RT | **$33** |
| You Are Always There For Me 163635, 1996 | General Line | OP | **$44** |
| You Are Always There For Me II 163600, 1997 | General Line | OP | **$55** |
| You Are My Amour (France) 456918, 1998 | Little Moments International | OP | **$35** |
| You Are My Christmas Special 104215, 2002 | General Line | YR | **$90** |
| You Are My Dream Come True 630026, 2007 | Bluebirds of Happiness | OP | **$55** |
| You Are My Favorite Dish 898457, 2002 | General Line | RT | **$29** |
| You Are My Favorite Dish 898457S, 2002 | General Line | RT | **$25** |
| You Are My Favorite Pastime PM0022, 2002 | Collectors' Club | * | **$40** |
| You Are My Favorite Star 527378, 1992 | General Line | RT | **$75** |
| You Are My Gift From Above 891738, 2002 | Family | OP | **$58** |
| You Are My Happiness 526185, 1990 | General Line | YR | **$44** |

You Are Always There For Me 163597, 1997, **$34.**

You Are Always There For Me
163619, 1997, **$48.**

You Are Always There For Me
163635, 1996, **$44.**

You Are My Happiness
526185, 1990, **$44.**

You Are My Main Event
115231, 1988, **$45.**

You Are Such a Purr-fect
Friend 524395, 1992, **$35.**

You Can Always Count on
Me 487953, 1999, **$32.**

| Title | Series | Limit | Trend |
|-------|--------|-------|-------|
| You Are My In-spa-ration PM0021, 2002 | Collectors' Club | * | **$41** |
| You Are My Main Event 115231, 1988 | Events | CL | **$45** |
| You Are My Main Event 115231 (Pink String Version), 1988 | Events | CL | **$60** |
| You Are My Mane Inspiration B0014, 1999 | Fun Club | CL | **$22** |
| You Are My Mane Inspiration B0114, 1999 | Birthday Club | CL | **$24** |
| You Are My Number One 520829, 1988 | General Line | SU | **$24** |
| You Are My Number One Friend 530026, 1993 | Easter Seals | CL | **$34** |
| You Are My Once In a Lifetime 531030, 1997 | General Line | RT | **$66** |
| You Are My Sunshine 710031, 2007 | General Line | OP | **$26** |
| You Are My Work of Art 640046, 2007 | General Line | 10,000 | **$45** |
| You Are Such a Heavenly Host 115625, 2003 | Catalog Exclusive | 5,000 | **$35** |
| You Are Such a Purr-fect Friend 524395, 1992 | General Line | OP | **$35** |

| Title | Series | Limit | Trend |
|---|---|---|---|
| You Are Such a Purr-fect Friend 526010, 1992 | Easter Seals | CL | **$616** |
| You Are Such a Purr-fect Friend 551001, 2006 | Musical | OP | **$15** |
| You Are the Apple of My Eye 115915, 2004 | Fruitful Delights | 7,500 | **$34** |
| You Are the Apple of My Eye-Yellow Apple 115915Y, 2004 | Fruitful Delights | * | **$50** |
| You Are the Cat's Meow 890952, 2001 | Special Wishes | SU | **$23** |
| You Are the End of My Rainbow C0014, 1994 | Collectors' Club | CL | **$29** |
| You Are the End of My Rainbow C0114, 1992 | Collectors' Club | CL | **$48** |
| You Are the Queen of My Heart 795151, 2001 | General Line | CL | **$50** |
| You Are the Rose In My Bouquet 103176, 2002 | Rose Petals Series/ GoCollect Exclusive | CL | **$68** |
| You Are the Rose of His Creation 531243, 1994 | Easter Seals | CL | **$560** |
| You Are the Sunshine of My Life 114013, 2004 | Special Wishes | OP | **$32** |

| Title | Series | Limit | Trend |
|---|---|---|---|
| You Are the Type I Love 523542, 1990 | General Line | RT | **$34** |
| You Are the Wind Beneath My Wings 795267, 2001 | Special Wishes | SU | **$35** |
| You Arrr a Treasure to Me 114026, 2004 | General Line | OP | **$45** |
| You Bet Your Boots I Love You 120121, 2004 | General Line | RT | **$26** |
| You Brighten My Field of Dreams 587850, 1999 | Country Lane | RT | **$49** |
| You Bring Me Out of My Shell 108546, 2003 | Sea of Friendship | OP | **$45** |
| You Can Always Bring a Friend 527122, 1991 | Events | CL | **$31** |
| You Can Always Count On Me 487953, 1999 | General Line | RT | **$32** |
| You Can Always Count On Me 526827, 1996 | Easter Seals | RT | **$23** |
| You Can Always Fudge a Little During the Season 455792, 1998 | General Line | OP | **$30** |
| You Can Fly 12335, 1985 | General Line | SU | **$58** |
| You Cane Count On Me 104273, 2002 | General Line | 9,000 | **$35** |

| Title | Series | Limit | Trend |
|-------|--------|-------|-------|
| You Can't Beat the Red, White and Blue (U.S.A.) 456411, 1998 | Little Moments International | OP | **$25** |
| You Can't Hide From God 795194, 2001 | General Line | OP | **$19** |
| You Can't Run Away From God E0525, 1984+ | General Line | RT | **$95** |
| You Can't Run Away From God E0525 (Fish Decal), 1983 | General Line | RT | **$95** |
| You Can't Run Away From God E0525 (Fish Mark), 1983 | General Line | RT | **$85** |
| You Can't Run Away From God E0525 (No Mark) | General Line | RT | **$155** |
| You Can't Take It With You 488321, 1999 | General Line | RT | **$22** |
| You Color Our World With Loving, Caring and Sharing 644463, 1999 | Events | RT | **$29** |
| You Complete My Heart 681067, 2000 | General Line | SU | **$27** |
| You Count 488372, 1999 | Special Wishes | RT | **$32** |
| You Decorate My Life 881139, 2001 | Catalog Exclusive | CL | **$35** |

| Title | Series | Limit | Trend |
|---|---|---|---|
| You Deserve a Halo—Thank You 531693, 1996 | General Line | RT | **$40** |
| You Deserve An Ovation 520578, 1991 | Special Wishes | OP | **$35** |
| You Fill the Air With Giggles and Laughter FC790006, 2007 | Fun Club | CL | **$40** |
| You Fill the Pages of My Life 530980, 1994 | Collectors' Club | CL | **$32** |
| You Have a Certain Glow About You 113945, 2003 | General Line | OP | **$30** |
| You Have a Heart of Gold 890626, 2002 | General Line | OP | **$23** |
| You Have a Special Place In My Heart 737534, 2000 | General Line | CL | **$85** |
| You Have Mastered the Art of Caring 456276, 1998 | Catalog Exclusive | CL | **$41** |
| You Have Such a Special Way of Caring 320706, 1997 | Little Moments | OP | **$25** |
| You Have the Beary Best Heart 730254, 2001 | Events | CL | **$35** |

You Can Always Fudge a
Little During the Season
455792, 1998, **$30.**

You Can't Run Away From God E0525,
1983, **$85-$155.**

You Have a Heart of Gold
890626, 2002, **$23.**

You Have a Special Place in My Heart 737534, 2000, **$85.**

You Have Touched So Many Hearts 261084, 1997, **$34.**

You Have Touched So Many Hearts E2821, 1984, **$47.**

| Title | Series | Limit | Trend |
|---|---|---|---|
| You Have the Sweetest Heart 689548, 2000 | General Line | OP | **$23** |
| You Have the Sweetest Smile 120007, 2004 | General Line | CL | **$24** |
| You Have Touched So Many Hearts 112577, 1988 | Musical | SU | **$45** |
| You Have Touched So Many Hearts 261084, 1997 | Special Wishes | OP | **$34** |
| You Have Touched So Many Hearts 261084B, 2002 | Special Wishes | OP | **$36** |
| You Have Touched So Many Hearts 272485, 1996 | Baby Classics | RT | **$17** |
| You Have Touched So Many Hearts 523283, 1990 | Easter Seals | RT | **$621** |
| You Have Touched So Many Hearts 527661, 1982 | General Line | SU | **$35** |
| You Have Touched So Many Hearts 551002, 2006 | Musical | CL | **$15** |
| You Have Touched So Many Hearts E2821, 1984 | General Line | SU | **$47** |
| You Just Cannot Chuck a Good Friendship PM882, 1988 | Collectors' Club | CL | **$43** |
| You Just Can't Replace a Good Friendship 488054, 1999 | General Line | OP | **$30** |

| Title | Series | Limit | Trend |
|---|---|---|---|
| You Light Up My Holly-Days 4003165, 2005 | General Line | OP | **$40** |
| You Make a World of Difference CC790002, 2007 | Collectors' Club | OP | **$40** |
| You Make My Heart Soar 118316, 2004 | Collectors' Club | OP | **$45** |
| You Make My Spirit Soar 139564, 1996 | Little Moments | OP | **$13** |
| You Make Such a Lovely Pair 531588, 1998 | Gcc Exclusive | RT | **$33** |
| You Make the Best of a Rainy Day 720018, 2007 | General Line | OP | **$65** |
| You Make the Grade 720001, 2007 | General Line | OP | **$35** |
| You Make the World a Sweeter Place 139521, 1996 | Little Moments | OP | **$33** |
| You Mean the Moose to Me 488038, 2000 | Birthday Train | OP | **$23** |
| You Melt My Heart 630002, 2007 | General Line | OP | **$27** |
| You Must Be Tickled Pink 550009, 2006 | General Line | OP | **$36** |
| You Oughta Be In Pictures 490327, 1999 | Events | SU | **$24** |

| Title | Series | Limit | Trend |
|---|---|---|---|
| You Set My Heart Ablaze 320625, 1997 | Little Moments | OP | **$18** |
| You Shall Receive a Crown of Glory 113965, 2003 | Special Wishes | RT | **$32** |
| You Should Be As Proud As a Peacock—Congratulations 733008, 2000 | Special Wishes | OP | **$26** |
| You Sparkle With Grace and Charm 620008, 2006 | General Line | OP | **$23** |
| You Suit Me to a Tee 526193, 1994 | General Line | RT | **$35** |
| You Sweep Me off My Feet 550008, 2006 | General Line | OP | **$45** |
| You Take the Cake 4004986, 2005 | General Line | OP | **$45** |
| You Tug On My Heart Strings 795526, 2001 | Boys & Girls Clubs of America | YR | **$48** |
| You Were Made For Me 4004375, 2005 | General Line | OP | **$27** |
| You Will Always Be a Treasure to Me PM971, 1997 | Collectors' Club | CL | **$44** |
| You Will Always Be Mine 795186, 2001 | General Line | OP | **$40** |
| You Will Always Be My Choice PM891, 1989 | Collectors' Club | CL | **$32** |

| Title | Series | Limit | Trend |
|-------|--------|-------|-------|
| You Will Always Be Our Hero 136271, 1995 | General Line | CL | **$41** |
| You'll Always Be a Winner to Me 272612, 1997 | Little Moments | OP | **$20** |
| You'll Always Be a Winner to Me 283460, 1997 | Little Moments | OP | **$20** |
| You'll Always Be Daddy's Little Girl 488224, 2000 | General Line | OP | **$45** |
| Your Comfort Comes From the Heart 720002, 2007 | General Line | OP | **$35** |
| Your Friendship Brightens Each Day 619002, 2006 | General Line | OP | **$40** |
| Your Friendship Grows Sweeter With Each Day 720011, 2007 | General Line | OP | **$40** |
| Your Friendship Sweetens My Life 720013, 2007 | General Line | OP | **$55** |
| Your Future Is So Rosy 550032, 2007 | General Line | OP | **$40** |
| Your Heart Is Forever Mine 4003778, 2005 | General Line | OP | **$36** |
| Your Kindness Will Not Be Forgotten 531197, 2002 | Nativity | * | **$45** |
| Your Love Fills My Heart 108522, 2003 | General Line | LE | **$45** |

| Title | Series | Limit | Trend |
|---|---|---|---|
| Your Love Gives Me Wings 610070, 2006 | General Line | LE | **$90** |
| Your Love Is Just So Comforting 104268, 2002 | General Line | OP | **$32** |
| Your Love Is So Uplifting 520675, 1988 | General Line | RT | **$90** |
| Your Love Keeps Me Toasty Warm 788031, 2000 | Catalog Exclusive | CL | **$36** |
| Your Love Makes My Heart Blossom 630008, 2007 | General Line | OP | **$40** |
| Your Love Means the World to Me 111896, 2004 | General Line | OP | **$34** |
| Your Love Reigns Forever In My Heart 115248, 2003 | Chapel Exclusive | OP | **$55** |
| Your Love Reigns Forever In My Heart 4004985, 2005 | General Line | OP | **$34** |
| Your Precious Spirit Comes Shining Through—Indianapolis 212563A, 1996 | General Line | YR | **$110** |
| Your Precious Spirit Comes Shining Through—Knoxville 212563, 1996 | General Line | YR | **$110** |
| Your Precious Spirit Comes Shining Through—Minneapolis 212563B, 1996 | General Line | YR | **$106** |

You Have Touched So
Many Hearts 272485, Baby
Classics series, 1996, **$17.**

Your Love is Just So Comforting
104268, 2002, **$32.**

You Melt My Heart 630002,
2007, **$27.**

You Take the Cake
4004986, 2005, **$45.**

| Title | Series | Limit | Trend |
|---|---|---|---|
| Your Song Fills the Air With Love CC790004, 2007 | Collectors' Club | * | **$50** |
| Your Spirit Glitters From Within 620006, 2006 | General Line | OP | **$32** |
| Your Spirit Is An Inspiration 104802, 2002 | Special Wishes | OP | **$23** |
| You're 1st In My Heart BC962, 1996 | Birthday Club | CL | **$23** |
| You're a Computer Cutie PM0012, 2001 | Collectors' Club | * | **$35** |
| You're a Dandy Mom and I'm Not Lion 795232V, 2001 | General Line | RT | **$37** |
| You're a Gem of a Friend 112882, 2003 | General Line | OP | **$34** |
| You're a Honey 795283, 2000 | General Line | SU | **$32** |
| You're a Life Saver to Me 204854, 1996 | General Line | RT | **$35** |
| You're a Perfect 10 104800, 2002 | Special Wishes | OP | **$25** |
| You're a Real Barbe-cutie 742872, 2002 | Special Wishes | OP | **$32** |
| You're An All-Star Graduate (Blonde) 101498, 2002 | General Line | OP | **$23** |
| You're An All-Star Graduate (Brunette) 101499, 2002 | General Line | OP | **$23** |

| Title | Series | Limit | Trend |
|---|---|---|---|
| You're A-peeling to Me 115914, 2004 | Fruitful Delights | 7,500 | **$34** |
| You're As Pretty As a Christmas Tree 530425, 1994 | Christmas Annual | SU | **$24** |
| You're As Pretty As a Christmas Tree 604216, 1994 | General Line | SU | **$35** |
| You're As Pretty As a Picture C0016, 1996 | Collectors' Club | CL | **$24** |
| You're As Pretty As a Picture C0116, 1996 | Collectors' Club | CL | **$33** |
| You're As Sweet As Apple Pie 795275, 2001 | General Line | SU | **$43** |
| You're Due For a Lifetime of Happiness 114015, 2003 | General Line | OP | **$34** |
| You're Forever In My Heart 139548, 1996 | Little Moments | OP | **$25** |
| You're Just As Sweet As Pie 307017, 1998 | Country Lane | RT | **$42** |
| You're Just Peachy 115918, 2004 | Fruitful Delights | 7,500 | **$34** |
| You're Just Perfect In My Book 320560, 1997 | Little Moments | OP | **$25** |
| You're Just Too Sweet to Be Scary 183849, 1997 | General Line | RT | **$48** |

You're a Dandy Mom and I'm
Not Lion 795232V, 2001, **$37.**

You're as Pretty as a Christmas
Tree 530425, Christmas Annual,
1994, **$24.**

You're As Pretty As a Picture
C0016, Precious Moments
Collectors' Club, 1996, **$24.**

You're As Sweet As Apple Pie
795275, 2001, **$43.**

You're Just Perfect in My Book 320560, Little Moments, 1997, **$25**

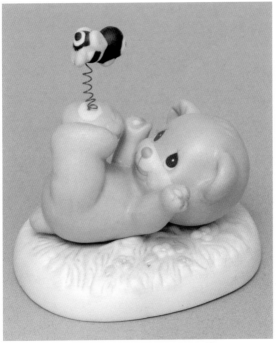

You're My Honey Bee 487929, 1999, **$20.**

| Title | Series | Limit | Trend |
|-------|--------|-------|-------|
| You're Just Too Thweet box 797693, 2002 | General Line | OP | **$21** |
| You're My Hero 720003, 2007 | General Line | OP | **$35** |
| You're My Honey Bee 487929, 1999 | General Line | RT | **$20** |
| You're My Mouseketeer 4004157, 2006 | Disney Showcase Collection | OP | **$32** |
| You're No. 1 Boy Figurine 491640, 1998 | Little Moments | OP | **$18** |
| You're No. 1 Girl Figurine 491624, 1998 | Little Moments | OP | **$18** |
| You're O.K. Buy Me 104267, 2002 | General Line | OP | **$34** |
| You're One In a Million to Me PM951, 1995 | Collectors' Club | CL | **$31** |
| You're Pear-fectly Sweet 115917, 2004 | Fruitful Delights | 7,500 | **$38** |
| You're Purr-fect, Pumpkin! 0000367, 2005 | General Line | OP | **$34** |

| Title | Series | Limit | Trend |
|-------|--------|-------|-------|
| You're So Bear-y Cool FC023, 2002 | Fun Club | CL | **$27** |
| You're the Berry Best 139513, 1996 | Little Moments | OP | **$18** |
| You're the Best Friend On the Block 524018, 2002 | General Line | SU | **$45** |
| You're the Cymbal of Perfection 4003177, 2005 | Nativity | OP | **$32** |
| You're the Sweetest Cookie In the Batch C0015, 1995 | Collectors' Club | CL | **$35** |
| You're the Sweetest Cookie In the Batch C0115, 1995 | Collectors' Club | CL | **$37** |
| You're Worth Your Weight In Gold E9282, 1983 | General Line | SU | **$30** |
| You're Worth Your Weight In Gold E9282B, 1988 | General Line | SU | **$30** |
| You've Made An Impression On Me 119434, 2004 | Special Wishes | OP | **$34** |

May Your Christmas Be Delightful ball ornament 114982, 2003, **$11.**

# ORNAMENTS

| Title | Series | Limit | Trend |
|---|---|---|---|
| 15 Years—Tweet Music Together 530840, 1992 | General Line | CL | **$25** |
| 20 Years and the Vision's Still the Same 451312, 1998 | General Line | CL | **$23** |
| Always Room For One More 522961, 1989 | Collectors' Club | RT | **$100** |
| Angel of Mercy 102407, 1985 | General Line | SU | **$19** |
| Baby Boy Waterball 118568, 2004 | General Line | YR | **$26** |
| Baby Boy's First Christmas Bootie 112182, 2003 | General Line | YR | **$26** |
| Baby Boy's First Christmas Waterball 112183, 2003 | General Line | YR | **$26** |
| Baby Girl Waterball 118569, 2004 | General Line | YR | **$26** |
| Baby Girl's First Christmas Bootie 112176, 2003 | General Line | YR | **$26** |
| Baby's First Chrismtas Girl Bootie 118527, 2004 | General Line | YR | **$26** |
| Baby's First Christmas 102504, 1986 | General Line | YR | **$25** |

| Title | Series | Limit | Trend |
|---|---|---|---|
| Baby's First Christmas 102512, 1986 | General Line | YR | **$23** |
| Baby's First Christmas 104204, 2002 | General Line | YR | **$20** |
| Baby's First Christmas 109401, 1987 | General Line | YR | **$65** |
| Baby's First Christmas 109428, 1987 | General Line | YR | **$35** |
| Baby's First Christmas 115282, 1988 | General Line | CL | **$25** |
| Baby's First Christmas 142719, 1995 | General Line | SU | **$20** |
| Baby's First Christmas 142727, 1995 | General Line | SU | **$20** |
| Baby's First Christmas 15903, 1985 | General Line | RT | **$30** |
| Baby's First Christmas 15911, 1985 | General Line | CL | **$30** |
| Baby's First Christmas 272744, 1997 | General Line | SU | **$21** |
| Baby's First Christmas 272752, 1997 | General Line | SU | **$21** |
| Baby's First Christmas 455644, 1998 | General Line | YR | **$20** |

| Title | Series | Limit | Trend |
|-------|--------|-------|-------|
| Baby's First Christmas 520241, 1988 | General Line | CL | **$25** |
| Baby's First Christmas 523194, 1989 | General Line | RT | **$25** |
| Baby's First Christmas 523208, 1989 | General Line | CL | **$25** |
| Baby's First Christmas 523771, 1990 | General Line | CL | **$20** |
| Baby's First Christmas 523798, 1990 | General Line | YR | **$28** |
| Baby's First Christmas 527475, 1992 | General Line | SU | **$27** |
| Baby's First Christmas 527483, 1992 | General Line | SU | **$23** |
| Baby's First Christmas 530255, 1994 | General Line | SU | **$18** |
| Baby's First Christmas 530263, 1994 | General Line | SU | **$30** |
| Baby's First Christmas 530859, 1992 | General Line | SU | **$21** |
| Baby's First Christmas 530867, 1992 | General Line | YR | **$25** |
| Baby's First Christmas 587826, 1999 | General Line | YR | **$23** |

| Title | Series | Limit | Trend |
|---|---|---|---|
| Baby's First Christmas 587834, 1999 | General Line | YR | **$23** |
| Baby's First Christmas Boy 104204, 2002 | General Line | YR | **$20** |
| Baby's First Christmas Boy 112843, 2003 | General Line | YR | **$30** |
| Baby's First Christmas Boy 117787, 2004 | General Line | YR | **$20** |
| Baby's First Christmas Boy 183946, 1996 | General Line | SU | **$20** |
| Baby's First Christmas Boy 4024080, 2005 | General Line | OP | **$20** |
| Baby's First Christmas Boy 455652, 1998 | General Line | SU | **$36** |
| Baby's First Christmas Boy 527084, 1991 | General Line | SU | **$25** |
| Baby's First Christmas Boy 610006, 2006 | General Line | * | **$40** |
| Baby's First Christmas Boy 730106, 2000 | General Line | CL | **$42** |
| Baby's First Christmas Boy 877506, 2001 | General Line | CL | **$19** |
| Baby's First Christmas Boy Bootie 118526, 2004 | General Line | YR | **$26** |

| Title | Series | Limit | Trend |
|---|---|---|---|
| Baby's First Christmas E2362, 1982 | General Line | SU | **$165** |
| Baby's First Christmas E2372, 1982 | General Line | SU | **$48** |
| Baby's First Christmas E5631, 1980 | General Line | SU | **$34** |
| Baby's First Christmas E5632, 1980 | General Line | SU | **$34** |
| Baby's First Christmas Girl 104206, 2002 | General Line | YR | **$20** |
| Baby's First Christmas Girl 112842, 2003 | General Line | YR | **$30** |
| Baby's First Christmas Girl 117788, 2004 | General Line | YR | **$20** |
| Baby's First Christmas Girl 183938, 1996 | General Line | SU | **$20** |
| Baby's First Christmas Girl 4024081, 2005 | General Line | YR | **$20** |
| Baby's First Christmas Girl 455644, 1998 | General Line | YR | **$33** |
| Baby's First Christmas Girl 527092, 1991 | General Line | CL | **$25** |
| Baby's First Christmas Girl 610005, 2006 | General Line | * | **$40** |

| Title | Series | Limit | Trend |
|---|---|---|---|
| Baby's First Christmas Girl 730092, 2000 | General Line | CL | **$19** |
| Baby's First Christmas Girl 877514, 2001 | General Line | CL | **$19** |
| Baby's First Christmas Snow-boots Boy 782238, 2000 | General Line | CL | **$26** |
| Baby's First Christmas Snow-boots Girl 782211, 2000 | General Line | CL | **$10** |
| Bear the Good News of Christmas 104515, 1987 | General Line | SU | **$25** |
| Beary Warm Aloha, A 101550, 2002 | Century Circle | CL | **$29** |
| Bea-ver-y Good This Year 117790, 2004 | General Line | YR | **$20** |
| Birds of a Feather Collect Together PM864, 1986 | Collectors' Club | CL | **$135** |
| Blessed Are the Meek PM390, 1990 | Collectors' Club | CL | **$20** |
| Blessed Are the Merciful PM590, 1990 | Collectors' Club | CL | **$20** |
| Blessed Are the Peacemakers PM790, 1990 | Collectors' Club | CL | **$20** |
| Blessed Are the Poor In Spirit PM190, 1990 | Collectors' Club | * | **$20** |
| Blessed Are the Pure In Heart E0518, 1983 | General Line | YR | **$40** |

| Title | Series | Limit | Trend |
|---|---|---|---|
| Blessed Are the Pure In Heart E5392, 1984 | General Line | CL | **$34** |
| Blessed Are the Pure In Heart PM690, 1990 | Collectors' Club | * | **$20** |
| Blessed Are They That Hunger PM490, 1990 | Collectors' Club | YR | **$20** |
| Blessed Are They That Mourn PM290, 1990 | Collectors' Club | YR | **$20** |
| Blessed With a Loving God-mother 4024104, 2005 | General Line | OP | **$20** |
| Boy and Puppy hinged hanging ornament 863181, 2001 | General Line | CL | **$26** |
| Bringing Bouquets of Love 104790, 2002 | General Line | SU | **$19** |
| Bringing You a Merry Christmas 528226, 1994 | General Line | RT | **$20** |
| Bundles of Joy 525057, 1989 | General Line | CL | **$27** |
| But Love Goes On Forever Girl E5628, 1980 | General Line | SU | **$110** |
| But Love Goes On Forever Girl E5628, 1984-1985 | General Line | SU | **$75** |
| But Love Goes On Forever Girl E5628 (Fish Mark), 1983 | General Line | SU | **$75** |
| But Love Goes On Forever Girl E5628 (Hourglass Mark), 1982 | General Line | SU | **$105** |

| Title | Series | Limit | Trend |
|---|---|---|---|
| But Love Goes On Forever Girl E5628 (Triangle Mark), 1981 | General Line | SU | **$115** |
| But Loves Goes On Forever Boy E5627, 1980 | General Line | SU | **$95** |
| But Loves Goes On Forever Boy E5627, 1984-1985 | General Line | SU | **$75** |
| But Loves Goes On Forever Boy E5627 (Fish Mark), 1983 | General Line | SU | **$75** |
| But Loves Goes On Forever Boy E5627 (Hourglass Mark), 1982 | General Line | SU | **$95** |
| But Loves Goes On Forever Boy E5627 (Triangle Mark), 1981 | General Line | SU | **$95** |
| But the Greatest of These Is Love 527696, 1992 | General Line | SU | **$34** |
| But the Greatest of These Is Love 527734, 1992 | General Line | CL | **$40** |
| Camel, Donkey and Cow (3-pc. set) E2386, 1982 | General Line | SU | **$90** |
| Cane You Join Us For a Merry Christmas 272698, 1997 | General Line | SU | **$35** |
| Cane You Join Us For a Merry Christmas Ball 272728, 1997 | General Line | SU | **$34** |

| Title | Series | Limit | Trend |
|---|---|---|---|
| Celebrating a Decade of Loving, Caring and Sharing 227986, 1990 | Collectors' Club | CL | **$12** |
| Chapel 530484, 1993 | Sugar Town | YR | **$23** |
| Cheers to the Leader 113999, 1988 | General Line | SU | **$30** |
| Christmas Bells Are Ringing 610026, 2006 | General Line | OP | **$20** |
| Christmas Is Ruff Without You 520462, 1988 | General Line | YR | **$36** |
| Christmas Is Something to Roar About 521116, 1998 | Birthday Train | SU | **$15** |
| Christmas Keeps Looking Up 521124, 1998 | Birthday Train | SU | **$15** |
| Christmas Together 610008, 2006 | General Line | OP | **$25** |
| Club That's Out of This World, The PM038, 1992 | Collectors' Club | CL | **$60** |
| Collecting Life's Most Precious Moments 108532, 2003 | 25th Anniversary | YR | **$25** |
| Come Let Us Adore Him (set of 4) E5633, 1981 | Nativity | SU | **$145** |
| Couple On Stump 118774, 2004 | General Line | YR | **$13** |
| Dashing Through the Snow 521574, 1987 | General Line | SU | **$24** |

| Title | Series | Limit | Trend |
|---|---|---|---|
| Daughter, You Bring Me Joy 610030, 2006 | General Line | OP | **$20** |
| Daughter, You'll Always Be My Princess 4024103, 2005 | General Line | OP | **$20** |
| Delivering Lots of Love 104789, 2002 | General Line | OP | **$28** |
| Don't Let the Holidays Get You Down 521590, 1988 | General Line | RT | **$25** |
| Dream Is a Wish Your Heart Makes, A 690016, | Disney Showcase Collection | OP | **$25** |
| Dropping In For Christmas E2369, 1982 | General Line | RT | **$50** |
| Dropping Over For Christmas E2376, 1984-1985 | General Line | RT | **$35** |
| Dropping Over For Christmas E2376 (Fish Mark), 1983 | General Line | RT | **$45** |
| Dropping Over For Christmas E2376 (Hourglass Mark), 1982 | General Line | RT | **$55** |
| Eight Mice a Milking 456055, 1999 | General Line | OP | **$20** |
| Even the Heavens Shall Praise Him 475084, 1998 | Century Circle | RT | **$30** |
| Event Filled With Sunshine and Smiles, An 160334, 1995 | General Line | SU | **$65** |

| Title | Series | Limit | Trend |
|---|---|---|---|
| Event Filled With Sunshine and Smiles, An 160334B, 1995 | General Line | SU | **$130** |
| Event Filled With Sunshine and Smiles, An 160334D, 1995 | General Line | SU | **$70** |
| Event Filled With Sunshine and Smiles, An 160334E, 1995 | General Line | SU | **$75** |
| Event Filled With Sunshine and Smiles, An 160334F, 1995 | General Line | SU | **$55** |
| Event Filled With Sunshine and Smiles, An 160334G, 1995 | General Line | SU | **$90** |
| Event Filled With Sunshine and Smiles, An 160334H, 1995 | General Line | SU | **$98** |
| Event For All Seasons, An 529974, 1993 | General Line | RT | **$20** |
| Event For All Seasons, An 530158, 1993 | General Line | SU | **$65** |
| Everything's Better With a Friend 690017 | Disney Showcase Collection | OP | **$25** |
| First Noel, The E2367, 1982 | General Line | SU | **$54** |
| First Noel, The E2368 (Cross Mark), 1984 | General Line | RT | **$50** |

| Title | Series | Limit | Trend |
|---|---|---|---|
| First Noel, The E2368 (Fish Mark), 1983 | General Line | RT | **$55** |
| First Noel, The E2368 (Hourglass Mark), 1982 | General Line | RT | **$60** |
| Friends Never Drift Apart 522937, 1989 | General Line | RT | **$27** |
| Future Is In Our Hands Basket, The 748986, 2000 | General Line | CL | **$25** |
| Future Is In Our Hands Holly 748994, 2000 | General Line | CL | **$28** |
| Future Is In Our Hands, The 730076, 2000 | General Line | CL | **$30** |
| Girl and Sled hinged hanging ornament 863203, 2001 | General Line | CL | **$26** |
| Girl and Tree hinged hanging ornament 863246, 2001 | General Line | CL | **$26** |
| Girl With Cocoa 117771, 2004 | General Line | OP | **$26** |
| Girl With Lamb 749087, 2000 | General Line | CL | **$26** |
| Girl With Patchwork Quilt 4003309, 2005 | General Line | YR | **$13** |
| Girl With Patchwork Quilt 4003310, 2005 | General Line | YR | **$10** |
| Give Your Whole Heart 634751, 1999 | Easter Seals | CL | **$33** |

| Title | Series | Limit | Trend |
|---|---|---|---|
| Glide Through the Holidays 521566, 1988 | General Line | RT | **$31** |
| God Bless You This Christmas 521094, 1998 | Birthday Train | SU | **$15** |
| God Loveth a Cheerful Giver 110239, 2003 | 25th Anniversary | OP | **$25** |
| God Sent His Love 15768, 1985 | General Line | YR | **$26** |
| God Sent You Just In Time 113972, 1988 | General Line | SU | **$31** |
| God's Love Is Crystal Clear 879487, 2001 | Century Circle | CL | **$25** |
| God's Precious Gift 183881, 1996 | General Line | OP | **$20** |
| Golden Rings of Friendship, The 456020, 1999 | General Line | OP | **$20** |
| Good Friends Are For Always 524131, 1992 | General Line | RT | **$24** |
| Good Lord Always Delivers, The 527165, 1990 | General Line | SU | **$24** |
| Grandma, I'll Never Outgrow You 4024101, 2005 | General Line | OP | **$15** |
| Grandma, Your Love Keeps Me Warm 610035, 2006 | General Line | OP | **$20** |

| Title | Series | Limit | Trend |
|-------|--------|-------|-------|
| Grandma's Little Angel 4024105, 2005 | General Line | OP | **$20** |
| Growing Love 520349, 1988 | Collectors' Club | CL | **$70** |
| Guide Us to Thy Perfect Light 610025, 2006 | General Line | YR | **$25** |
| Hang On For the Holly Days 520292, 1988 | General Line | YR | **$27** |
| Hanging Out For the Holidays 104795, 2002 | General Line | SU | **$17** |
| Happiness Is the Lord 15830, 1985 | General Line | SU | **$28** |
| Happy Holi-daze 520454, 1998 | General Line | RT | **$19** |
| Happy Hula Days 118267, 2004 | General Line | * | **$20** |
| Happy Trails Is Trusting Jesus 523224, 1989 | General Line | SU | **$23** |
| Hatching the Perfect Holiday 456039, 1999 | General Line | OP | **$20** |
| Have a Heavenly Christmas 12416, 1984 | General Line | RT | **$35** |
| He Cleansed My Soul 112380, 1986 | General Line | RT | **$19** |
| He Covers the Earth With His Beauty 142662, 1995 | General Line | CL | **$27** |

| Title | Series | Limit | Trend |
|---|---|---|---|
| He Covers the Earth With His Beauty 142689, 1995 | General Line | SU | **$39** |
| Heaven Bless Your Special Christmas 521086, 1998 | Birthday Train | SU | **$15** |
| Hippo Holidays 520403, 1995 | General Line | SU | **$25** |
| Holiday Surprises Come In All Sizes 104793, 2002 | General Line | OP | **$19** |
| Home For the Holidays PMb225, 2001 | Collectors' Club | * | **$25** |
| Home Sweet Home Ball 104208, 2002 | General Line | YR | **$30** |
| Honk If You Love Jesus 15857, 1985 | General Line | SU | **$20** |
| Hooked On the Holidays 104794, 2002 | General Line | SU | **$17** |
| House 530468, 1994 | Sugar Town | YR | **$14** |
| How Can Two Work Together Except They Agree 456268, 1998 | Care-A-Van | CL | **$25** |
| I Believe In the Old Rugged Cross 522953, 1988 | General Line | SU | **$26** |
| I Can't Give You Anything But Love 4024106, 2005 | General Line | OP | **$20** |
| Ice See You a Champion 934852, 2002 | Canadian Exclusive | LE | **$25** |

| Title | Series | Limit | Trend |
|-------|--------|-------|-------|
| Ice Skating Girl 117768, 2004 | General Line | OP | **$26** |
| Icy Good Times Ahead 112138, 2003 | General Line | YR | **$18** |
| Icy Good Times Ahead 112141, 2003 | General Line | YR | **$26** |
| Icy Good Times Ahead 112142, 2003 | General Line | YR | **$26** |
| Icy Good Times Ahead 112145, 2003 | General Line | YR | **$25** |
| I-Cy Good Times Ahead 112840, 2003 | General Line | YR | **$20** |
| I-Cy Potential In You 112875, 2003 | General Line | YR | **$45** |
| I'll Be Dog-ged It's That Season Again 455660, 1998 | General Line | SU | **$22** |
| I'll Play My Drum For Him E2359, 1982 | General Line | YR | **$100** |
| I'm a Possibility 111120, 1986 | General Line | SU | **$36** |
| I'm Just Nutty About the Holidays 455776, 1998 | General Line | RT | **$19** |
| I'm Nuts About You 520411, 1992 | General Line | CL | **$24** |
| I'm Sending You a Merry Christmas 455628, 1998 | General Line | SU | **$29** |

| Title | Series | Limit | Trend |
|---|---|---|---|
| I'm Sending You a White Christmas 112372, 1986 | General Line | SU | **$17** |
| In God's Beautiful Garden of Love 261599, 1997 | Century Circle | CL | **$150** |
| It Is No Secret What God Can Do 244570, 1994 | Easter Seals | YR | **$10** |
| It's a Perfect Boy 102415, 1985 | General Line | SU | **$27** |
| It's So Uplifting to Have a Friend Like You 528846, 1992 | General Line | RT | **$20** |
| Jesus Is the Light That Shines E0537, 1983 | General Line | SU | **$70** |
| Joy From Head to Mistletoe 150126, 1995 | General Line | OP | **$19** |
| Joy to the World 1st Issue 150320, 1995 | Joy to the World | RT | **$25** |
| Joy to the World 2nd Issue 153338, 1996 | Joy to the World | RT | **$25** |
| Joy to the World 3rd Issue 272566, 1997 | Joy to the World | RT | **$24** |
| Joy to the World E2343, 1982 | General Line | SU | **$36** |
| Joy to the World E5388, 1984 | General Line | RT | **$36** |
| Kid and Snowman hinged hanging ornament 863173, 2001 | General Line | OP | **$26** |

| Title | Series | Limit | Trend |
|-------|--------|-------|-------|
| Kid, Tree and hinged hanging ornament 863211, 2001 | General Line | CL | **$26** |
| Legend of Gifts, The, 529451, 2004 | General Line | OP | **$20** |
| Legend of Holly, The 531820, 2004 | General Line | OP | **$20** |
| Legend of the Candy Cane, The 532193, 2004 | General Line | OP | **$20** |
| Legend of the Christmas Tree, The 528676, 2004 | General Line | OP | **$20** |
| Legend of the Pointsettia, The 531863, 2004 | General Line | OP | **$20** |
| Legend of the Wreath, The 529532, 2004 | General Line | OP | **$20** |
| Let Earth Receive Her King 748390, 2000 | Chapel Exclusive | OP | **$25** |
| Let Heaven and Nature Sing E0532, 1983-1986 | General Line | RT | **$35** |
| Let the Heavens Rejoice E5629 (Triangle Mark), 1981 | General Line | YR | **$205** |
| Let the Heavens Rejoice E5629 (Triangle Mark, No Patch), 1981 | General Line | YR | **$260** |

| Title | Series | Limit | Trend |
|---|---|---|---|
| Let's Keep Our Eyes On the Goal 802557, 2001 | Canadian Exclusive | LE | **$20** |
| Lord Is Our Chief Inspiration, The 879738, 2001 | Chapel Exclusive | OP | **$20** |
| Lord Keep Me On My Toes 102423, 1985 | General Line | RT | **$31** |
| Lord Keep Me On My Toes 525332, 1992 | General Line | OP | **$22** |
| Love Is Kind E5391, 1984 | General Line | SU | **$35** |
| Love Is Patient E0535, 1983 | General Line | SU | **$58** |
| Love Is Patient E0536, 1983 | General Line | SU | **$68** |
| Love Is the Best Gift of All 109770, 1986 | General Line | YR | **$39** |
| Love Makes the World Go 'Round 184209, 1996 | General Line | SU | **$44** |
| Love Makes the World Go 'Round 184209P, 1996 | General Line | SU | **$23** |
| Love One Another 522929, 1989 | General Line | RT | **$25** |
| Love Rescued Me 102385, 1985 | General Line | RT | **$25** |
| Loving, Caring and Sharing Along the Way PM040, 1993 | Collectors' Club | CL | **$31** |

| Title | Series | Limit | Trend |
|-------|--------|-------|-------|
| Magic Starts With You, The 529648, 1992 | General Line | CL | **$16** |
| Make a Joyful Noise 522910, 1988 | General Line | SU | **$27** |
| Making the Holidays Special 104788, 2002 | General Line | * | **$19** |
| May All Your Christmases Be White 521302, 1988 | General Line | SU | **$29** |
| May All Your Christmases Be White 521302R, 1999 | General Line | SU | **$20** |
| May God Bless You With a Perfect Season E5390, 1984 | General Line | SU | **$33** |
| May Love Blossom All Around You 115925, 2004 | Century Circle | LE | **$20** |
| May the Holidays Keep You Bright-Eyed and Bushy Tailed 112876, 2003 | General Line | YR | **$27** |
| May Your Christmas Be a Happy Home 523704, 1989 | General Line | CL | **$32** |
| May Your Christmas Be Delightful 114982, 2003 | Avon Exclusive | YR | **$11** |
| May Your Christmas Be Delightful 15849, 1985 | General Line | SU | **$38** |
| May Your Christmas Be Delightful 15849R, 1999 | General Line | SU | **$20** |

| Title | Series | Limit | Trend |
|---|---|---|---|
| May Your Christmas Be Delightful 587931, 1999 | General Line | CL | **$20** |
| May Your Christmas Be Gigantic 521108, 1998 | Birthday Train | SU | **$15** |
| May Your Christmas Be Happy 15822, 1985 | General Line | SU | **$45** |
| May Your Christmas Be Merry 524174, 1991 | General Line | SU | **$35** |
| May Your Christmas Be Merry 526940, 1991 | General Line | SU | **$36** |
| May Your Christmas Be Warm Baby 470279, 1998 | Birthday Train | OP | **$15** |
| May Your Christmas Begin With a Bang 877441, 2001 | General Line | CL | **$26** |
| May Your Days Be Warm & Fuzzy 4004583, 2005 | General Line | YR | **$16** |
| May Your Holidays Be So-Sew Special 4003161, 2005 | General Line | YR | **$43** |
| May Your Holidays Be So-Sew Special 4003162, 2005 | General Line | YR | **$64** |
| May Your Holidays Sparkle With Joy 104203, 2002 | General Line | YR | **$20** |
| May Your Wishes For Peace Take Wing 587818, 1999 | General Line | CL | **$27** |

| Title | Series | Limit | Trend |
|-------|--------|-------|-------|
| Merry Chrismoose 150134, 1995 | General Line | SU | **$29** |
| Merry Christmas Little Lamb 521078, 1998 | Birthday Train | SU | **$15** |
| Merry Giftness 532223, 1999 | General Line | CL | **$20** |
| Most Precious Gift of Them All, The 212520, 1996 | General Line | SU | **$23** |
| Mother Sew Dear E0514, 1983+ | General Line | RT | **$10-$30** |
| Mother Sew Dear E0514 (Stamped Fish Mark), 1983 | General Line | RT | **$55** |
| Mouse With Cheese E2381, 1982 | General Line | SU | **$117** |
| My Godmother, My Guiding Light 610033, 2006 | General Line | OP | **$20** |
| My Happiness PM904, 1990 | Collectors' Club | CL | **$71** |
| My Love Will Keep You Warm 272965, 1997 | General Line | CL | **$25** |
| My Love Will Never Let You Go 114006, 1988 | General Line | SU | **$30** |
| My True Love Gave to Me 455989, 1998 | General Line | OP | **$32** |
| No One's Sweeter Than Mom 104785, 2002 | General Line | OP | **$19** |

No One's Sweeter Than Mom ornament 104785, 2002, **$19.**

| Title | Series | Limit | Trend |
|---|---|---|---|
| No Rest For the Weary 4024100, 2005 | General Line | OP | **$20** |
| Nurses Care For the Heart and Soul 610034, 2006 | General Line | OP | **$20** |
| Nurse's Care Is the Best Medicine, A 4024108, 2005 | General Line | OP | **$15** |
| O Come All Ye Faithful E0531, 1983 | General Line | SU | **$60** |
| Oh Holy Night 522848, 1988 | General Line | YR | **$35** |
| Once Upon a Holy Night 523852, 1989 | General Line | CL | **$27** |
| One Good Turn Deserves Another 737569, 2000 | General Line | OP | **$20** |
| Onward Christmas Soldiers 527327, 1994 | General Line | RT | **$19** |
| Ornaments (set of 7) PM890, 1990 | Collectors' Club | CL | **$100** |
| Our First Christmas Igloo 112185, 2003 | General Line | YR | **$25** |
| Our First Christmas Together 102350, 1986 | General Line | YR | **$25** |
| Our First Christmas Together 104207, 2002 | General Line | YR | **$25** |
| Our First Christmas Together 112399, 1987 | General Line | YR | **$29** |

| Title | Series | Limit | Trend |
|---|---|---|---|
| Our First Christmas Together 112841, 2003 | General Line | YR | **$25** |
| Our First Christmas Together 117786, 2004 | General Line | YR | **$25** |
| Our First Christmas Together 142700, 1995 | General Line | SU | **$21** |
| Our First Christmas Together 183911, 1996 | General Line | SU | **$24** |
| Our First Christmas Together 272736, 1997 | General Line | SU | **$25** |
| Our First Christmas Together 4003163, 2005 | General Line | YR | **$20** |
| Our First Christmas Together 455636, 1998 | General Line | SU | **$26** |
| Our First Christmas Together 520233, 1988 | General Line | CL | **$26** |
| Our First Christmas Together 521558, 1989 | General Line | SU | **$36** |
| Our First Christmas Together 522945, 1991 | General Line | CL | **$26** |
| Our First Christmas Together 525324, 1990 | General Line | CL | **$28** |
| Our First Christmas Together 528870, 1992 | General Line | SU | **$25** |

| Title | Series | Limit | Trend |
|---|---|---|---|
| Our First Christmas Together 529206, 1994 | General Line | CL | **$23** |
| Our First Christmas Together 530506, 1993 | General Line | SU | **$21** |
| Our First Christmas Together 587796, 1999 | General Line | CL | **$29** |
| Our First Christmas Together 730084, 2000 | General Line | CL | **$40** |
| Our First Christmas Together 878855, 2001 | General Line | CL | **$40** |
| Our First Christmas Together E2385, 1984+ | General Line | SU | **$25** |
| Our First Christmas Together E2385 (Fish Mark), 1983 | General Line | SU | **$45** |
| Our First Christmas Together E2385 (Hourglass Mark), 1982 | General Line | SU | **$50** |
| Overflowing With Holiday Joy 104792, 2002 | General Line | SU | **$19** |
| Owl Be Home For Christmas 128708, 1996 | Birthday Series | SU | **$20** |
| Pack Your Trunk For the Holidays 272949, 1997 | General Line | CL | **$25** |
| Packed With Love 104791, 2002 | General Line | SU | **$18** |

| Title | Series | Limit | Trend |
|---|---|---|---|
| Papas Make the Season Bright 104786, 2002 | General Line | OP | **$18** |
| Peace On Earth 177091, 1995 | Century Circle | 15,000 | **$27** |
| Peace On Earth 523062, 1989 | General Line | YR | **$40** |
| Peace On Earth 679259, 1999 | Gcc Exclusive | CL | **$25** |
| Peace On Earth E5389, 1984 | General Line | SU | **$20** |
| Peace On Earth...Anyway 183350, 1996 | General Line | SU | **$24** |
| Peace On Earth...Anyway 183369, 1996 | General Line | SU | **$21** |
| Perfect Grandpa, The E0517, 1983 | General Line | SU | **$33** |
| Pretty As a Princess 587958, 1999 | General Line | CL | **$20** |
| Puppy Pushing Sled 272892, 1997 | General Line | RT | **$23** |
| Purr-fect Gift, The 4024082, 2005 | General Line | OP | **$43** |
| Purr-fect Grandma, The E0516, 1983 | General Line | RT | **$30** |
| Purr-fect Grandpa, The E5017, 1983 | General Line | SU | **$30** |
| Reindeer 102466, 1986 | General Line | YR | **$144** |

| Title | Series | Limit | Trend |
|---|---|---|---|
| Rejoice O Earth 113980, 1988 | General Line | RT | **$16** |
| Remember the Sweetness of the Season 532193, 2004 | General Line | OP | **$16** |
| Ringing In the Season 456012, 1998 | General Line | OP | **$25** |
| Ringing In the Season 610002, 2006 | General Line | YR | **$20** |
| Ringing In the Season 610003, 2006 | General Line | YR | **$30** |
| Rocking Horse 102474, 1985 | General Line | SU | **$18** |
| Saying Oui to Our Love 456004, 1998 | General Line | OP | **$24** |
| Sending You a White Christmas 528218, 1994 | General Line | RT | **$18** |
| Serve With a Smile 102431, 1985 | General Line | SU | **$13** |
| Serve With a Smile 102458, 1985 | General Line | SU | **$20** |
| Serving Up Fun 4024110, 2005 | General Line | OP | **$18** |
| Shall I Play For You? 610029, 2006 | General Line | OP | **$18** |
| Share In the Warmth of Christmas 527211, 1992 | General Line | RT | **$19** |

| Title | Series | Limit | Trend |
|---|---|---|---|
| Sharing a Gift of Love 233196, 1990 | General Line | YR | **$10** |
| Sharing the Good News Together PM037, 1991 | Collectors' Club | CL | **$55** |
| Sharing the Light of Love 119204, 2004 | General Line | * | **$10** |
| Shepherd of Love 102288, 1985 | General Line | SU | **$26** |
| Sing a New Song 610028, 2006 | General Line | OP | **$18** |
| Sister, You Have a Heart of Gold 4024102, 2005 | General Line | OP | **$18** |
| Sister, You're An Angel to Me 610031, 2006 | General Line | OP | **$18** |
| Skiing Girl 117769, 2004 | Snow Sweeties | * | **$13** |
| Sledding Girl 117770, 2004 | Snow Sweeties | * | **$13** |
| Slide Into the Next Millennium With Joy 587788, 1999 | General Line | CL | **$28** |
| Slow Down and Enjoy the Holidays 520489, 1993 | General Line | YR | **$20** |
| Slow Down For the Holidays 272760, 1997 | Birthday Series | SU | **$17** |

| Title | Series | Limit | Trend |
|---|---|---|---|
| Smile Along the Way 113964, 1988 | General Line | SU | **$21** |
| S'mitten With the Christmas Spirit 117784, 2004 | General Line | YR | **$23** |
| S'mitten With the Christmas Spirit 117843, 2004 | General Line | YR | **$27** |
| Sno-ball Without You 520446, 2001 | General Line | CL | **$24** |
| Sno-bunny Falls For You Like I Do 520438, 1991 | General Line | CL | **$19** |
| Snowboarding Girl 117767, 2004 | Snow Sweeties | * | **$13** |
| Snowtubing Girl 117772, 2004 | Snow Sweeties | * | **$13** |
| Somebody Cares 272922, 1997 | Easter Seals | YR | **$8** |
| Sugar Town Doctor's Office 530441, 1995 | Sugar Town | RT | **$14** |
| Surround Us With Joy E0513, 1983 | General Line | YR | **$60** |
| Surrounded With Joy Girl 531685, 1993 | Chapel Exclusive | SU | **$24** |
| Sweet 16 266841, 1996 | Collectors' Club | * | **$300** |
| Swimming Into Your Heart 456047, 1998 | General Line | OP | **$20** |

| Title | Series | Limit | Trend |
|---|---|---|---|
| Take a Bow Cuz You're My Christmas Star 520470, 1994 | General Line | SU | **$24** |
| Take Time to Smell the Flowers 128899, 1995 | Easter Seals | CL | **$12** |
| Teacher, You're a Precious Work of Art 4024109, 2005 | General Line | OP | **$18** |
| Teachers Make the Season Bright 610032, 2006 | General Line | OP | **$18** |
| Tell Me the Story of Jesus E0533, 1983 | General Line | SU | **$36** |
| There's a Christian Welcome Here 528021, 1992 | Chapel Exclusive | YR | **$25** |
| There's Sno-one Like You 104209, 2002 | General Line | YR | **$19** |
| Thoughts of You Are So Heart-warming 117789, 2004 | General Line | YR | **$37** |
| Time to Wish You a Merry Christmas 115320, 1988 | General Line | YR | **$41** |
| To a Special Dad E0515, 1983 | General Line | SU | **$31** |
| To My Forever Friend 113956, 1988 | General Line | RT | **$24** |
| To Thee With Love E0534, 1984+ | General Line | RT | **$30** |
| To Thee With Love E0534 (Fish Mark), 1983 | General Line | RT | **$50** |
| Train Station 184101, 1996 | Sugar Town | RT | **$23** |

| Title | Series | Limit | Trend |
|-------|--------|-------|-------|
| Trumpet His Arrival 610027, 2006 | General Line | OP | **$20** |
| Trust and Obey 102377, 1986 | General Line | RT | **$24** |
| Unicorn E2371, 1982 | General Line | RT | **$60** |
| Universal Love 238899, 1990 | General Line | YR | **$12** |
| Unto Us a Child Is Born E5630, 1984-1985 | General Line | SU | **$40** |
| Unto Us a Child Is Born E5630 (Fish Mark), 1983 | General Line | SU | **$45** |
| Unto Us a Child Is Born E5630 (Hourglass Mark), 1982 | General Line | SU | **$45** |
| Unto Us a Child Is Born E5630 (No Mark), 1981 | General Line | SU | **$70** |
| Unto Us a Child Is Born E5630 (Triangle Mark), 1981 | General Line | SU | **$60** |
| Waddle I Do Without You 112364, 1986 | General Line | RT | **$18** |
| Warmed By Your Love 710020, 2007 | General Line | OP | **$20** |
| We Have Seen His Star E6120 (Cross Mark), 1984 | General Line | RT | **$50** |
| We Have Seen His Star E6120 (Fish Mark), 1983 | General Line | RT | **$55** |
| We Have Seen His Star E6120 (Hourglass Mark), 1982 | General Line | RT | **$60** |

| Title | Series | Limit | Trend |
|---|---|---|---|
| We Have Seen His Star E6120 (No Mark), 1981 | General Line | RT | **$65** |
| We Have Seen His Star E6120 (Triangle Mark), 1981 | General Line | RT | **$60** |
| Wee Three Kings E5634 (Cross Mark), 1984 | General Line | SU | **$105** |
| Wee Three Kings E5634 (Fish Mark), 1983 | General Line | SU | **$105** |
| Wee Three Kings E5634 (Hourglass Mark), 1982 | General Line | SU | **$110** |
| Wee Three Kings E5634 (Triangle Mark), 1981 | General Line | SU | **$150** |
| We're Two of a Kind 455997, 1998 | General Line | OP | **$30** |
| When the Skating's Ruff, Try Prayer 183903, 1996 | General Line | OP | **$20** |
| Winter Is So Cool 710023, 2007 | General Line | OP | **$16** |
| Winter Wishes Warm the Heart 184241, 2001 | Century Circle & Avon Exclusive | YR | **$46** |
| Winter's Such a Ball 710019, 2007 | General Line | OP | **$16** |
| Wishing Ewe Sweet Christmas Dreams 610007, 2006 | General Line | YR | **$20** |
| Wishing You a Bear-ie Merry Christmas 531200, 1996 | General Line | SU | **$14** |

| Title | Series | Limit | Trend |
|---|---|---|---|
| Wishing You a Cozy Christmas 102326, 1985 | General Line | YR | **$29** |
| Wishing You a Merry Christmas E5387, 1984 | General Line | YR | **$32** |
| Wishing You a Purr-fect Holiday 520497, 1989 | General Line | SU | **$22** |
| Wishing You the Sweetest Christmas 530190, 1993 | General Line | SU | **$23** |
| Wishing You the Sweetest Christmas 530212, 1993 | General Line | CL | **$33** |
| Worthy Is the Lamb 928577, 2002 | Chapel Exclusive | OP | **$19** |
| You Are Always In My Heart 530972, 1994 | General Line | SU | **$15** |
| You Are My Gift Come True 520276, 1988 | General Line | CL | **$16** |
| You Are the End of My Rainbow PM041, 1994 | Collectors' Club | CL | **$25** |
| You Can Always Count On Me 152579, 1995 | Easter Seals | YR | **$9** |
| You Cane Count On Me 104274, 2002 | Catalog Exclusive | CL | **$20** |
| You Decorate My Life 119203, 2004 | General Line | * | **$10** |
| You Decorate My Life 881147, 2001 | Catalog Exclusive | CL | **$30** |

| Title | Series | Limit | Trend |
|---|---|---|---|
| You Decorate My Life 881163, 2001 | General Line | RT | **$45** |
| You Have Touched So Many Hearts 112356, 1986 | General Line | RT | **$19** |
| You Were Made For Me 4004376, 2005 | General Line | OP | **$20** |
| You'll Always Be a Winner to Me 4024111, 2005 | General Line | OP | **$16** |
| Your Love Keeps Me Toasty Warm 795577, 2000 | Catalog Exclusive | CL | **$25** |
| Your Love Keeps Me Toasty Warm 800813, 2000 | Catalog Exclusive | CL | **$50** |
| Your Spirit Is An Inspiration 4024112, 2005 | General Line | OP | **$18** |
| You're "A" Number One In My Book, Teacher 150142, 1995 | General Line | RT | **$19** |
| You're a Gem of a Friend 4024107, 2005 | General Line | OP | **$18** |
| You're As Pretty As a Christmas Tree 530387, 1994 | General Line | YR | **$23** |
| You're As Pretty As a Christmas Tree 530395, 1994 | General Line | YR | **$28** |
| You're My Number One Friend 250112, 1993 | Easter Seals | CL | **$12** |
| You're One of a Kind 710024, 2007 | General Line | OP | **$16** |

# *Plates*

| Title | Series | Limit | Trend |
|-------|--------|-------|-------|
| Autumn's Praise 12122, 1986 | Four Seasons | 1,500 | **$38** |
| Blessings From Me to Thee 523860, 1991 | Christmas Blessings | CL | **$50** |
| Bring the Little Ones to Jesus 531359, 1994 | General Line | SU | **$37** |
| But the Greatest of These Is Love 527742, 1992 | Christmas Blessings | CL | **$50** |
| Cane You Join Us For a Merry Christmas 272701, 1997 | Beauty of Christmas | CL | **$53** |
| Chapel Lighted Plate 150304, | General Line | RT | **$87** |
| Christmastime Is For Sharing E-0505, 1983 | Joy of Christmas | YR | **$63** |
| Come Let Us Adore Him E5646, 1981 | Christmas | CL | **$47** |
| Future Is In Our Hands, The 749036, 2000 | General Line | CL | **$25** |
| Good Friends Are Forever 186457, 1996 | General Line | * | **$40** |

| Title | Series | Limit | Trend |
|-------|--------|-------|-------|
| Hand That Rocks the Future E9256, 1983 | Mother's Love | 15,000 | **$38** |
| He Covers the Earth With His Beauty 142670, 1995 | Beauty of Christmas | CL | **$48** |
| He Hath Made Everything Beautiful In His Time 129151, 1995 | Mother's Day | SU | **$45** |
| I Believe In Miracles E9257, 1983 | Inspired Thoughts | 15,000 | **$40** |
| I'll Play My Drum For Him E2357, 1982 | Joy of Christmas | YR | **$47** |
| I'm Sending You a White Christmas 101834, 1986 | Christmas Love | YR | **$49** |
| Jesus Loves Me E9275, 1982 | General Line | SU | **$37** |
| Jesus Loves Me E9276, 1982 | General Line | SU | **$37** |
| Let Heaven and Nature Sing E2347, 1982 | Christmas | 15,000 | **$45** |
| Lord Bless You and Keep You, The E5216, 1981 | General Line | SU | **$36** |
| Love Is Kind E2847, 1984 | Inspired Thoughts | CL | **$42** |
| Love One Another E5215, 1985 | Inspired Thoughts | 15,000 | **$48** |
| Loving Thy Neighbor E2848, 1984 | Mother's Day | RT | **$37** |

| Title | Series | Limit | Trend |
|-------|--------|-------|-------|
| Make a Joyful Noise E7174, 1982 | Inspired Thoughts | CL | **$43** |
| May Your Christmas Be a Happy Home 523003, 1989 | Christmas Love | YR | **$47** |
| May Your Holidays Sparkle 104058, 2002 | General Line | CL | **$26** |
| Merry Christmas Deer 520284, 1988 | Christmas Love | YR | **$54** |
| Mother Sew Dear E5217, 1980 | Mother's Love | RT | **$38** |
| My Peace I Give Unto Thee 102954, 1987 | Christmas Love | YR | **$44** |
| Of All the Mothers I Have Known, There's None As Precious As My Own 163716, 1996 | Mother's Day | YR | **$39** |
| Our First Christmas Together E2378, 1982 | General Line | SU | **$24** |
| Peace On Earth...Anyway 183377, 1996 | Beauty of Christmas | SU | **$42** |
| Precious Moments Last Forever Plaque 12246, 1984 | General Line | CL | **$140** |
| Purr-fect Grandma, The E7173, 1982 | Mother's Love | CL | **$36** |
| Rejoicing With You E7172, 1981 | General Line | SU | **$31** |

| Title | Series | Limit | Trend |
|---|---|---|---|
| Sugar Town Plate 150304, | Sugar Town | OP | **$79** |
| Summer's Joy 12114, 1985 | Four Seasons | YR | **$44** |
| Tell Me the Story of Jesus 15237, 1985 | Joy of Christmas | YR | **$55** |
| Thinking of You Is What I Really Like to Do 531766, 1993 | Mother's Day | SU | **$46** |
| Unto Us a Child Is Born E5395, 1984 | Christmas | CL | **$44** |
| Voice of Spring, The 12106, 1985 | Four Seasons | YR | **$49** |
| Wedding 4-Inch decorative plate 256730, 1996 | General Line | CL | **$26** |
| Wee Three Kings E0538, 1983 | Christmas | 15,000 | **$27** |
| Winter's Song 12130, 1986 | Four Seasons | YR | **$40** |
| Wishing You a Yummy Christmas 523801, 1990 | Christmas Blessings | CL | **$39** |
| Wishing You the Sweetest Christmas 530204, 1993 | Christmas Blessings | SU | **$52** |
| Wonder of Christmas, The E5396, 1984 | Joy of Christmas | YR | **$45** |
| You're As Pretty As a Christmas Tree 530409, 1994 | Beauty of Christmas | SU | **$47** |

# Numerical Index